MEGA BOOK

of

MINI CROSSWORDS

150 High-Speed 9×9 Puzzles

PUZZLE
WRIGHT
PRESS

New York

PUZZLE WRIGHT PRESS

New York

PUZZLEWRIGHT PRESS and the distinctive Puzzlewright Press logo
are registered trademarks of Sterling Publishing Co., Inc.

© 2023 Vox Media, LLC

The puzzles in this book originally appeared on the
Vox.com website between October 2020 and May 2021.

ISBN 978-1-4549-5005-9

For information about custom editions, special sales, and premium purchases,
please contact specialsales@unionsquareandco.com.

Manufactured in Canada

2 4 6 8 10 9 7 5 3 1

unionsquareandco.com

Cover design by Gavin Motnyk

CONTENTS

INTRODUCTION

Welcome, crossword solvers, to your daily dose of distraction. These Vox weekday puzzles provide just the right amount of brain challenge, the perfect dollop of whimsy, and an opportunity for a winning feeling every time you complete one. I like to think of the weekday puzzle as snackable, something you can pull up on your phone or tablet when you have a few minutes to yourself. Now, you can whip out this book, no Wi-Fi required, and lose yourself for a little while in a grid.

That's how one of Vox's crossword constructors, Juliana Tringali Golden, got hooked on crosswords. When her kids were little, she found she could pick up the daily New York Times puzzle on her phone and solve a few clues, over and over throughout the day. It provided some mental stimulation, and it lit a spark: She went on to become a crossword creator. Crosswords, she says, are "a great thing to be able to pick up and put down as time allows, and they're probably a better thing to do on our phones than, say, scrolling Twitter."

It seems many share her view: Tens of millions of people every day have picked up a pen or pencil or fired up a screen to solve a crossword puzzle. Vox puzzles, which debuted in 2019, now reach thousands of solvers daily. As for why crossword puzzles remain so popular, the creators agree that, well, games are fun! Or as another Vox puzzle constructor Patrick Blindauer says, "It feels good to figure things out."

The 9×9 weekday puzzles (mostly themed, but some themeless) that make up this book are brought to you by crossword creators Andrew J. Ries, Will Nediger, Adesina O. Koiki, Juliana Tringali Golden, and Patrick Blindauer. These folks keep our daily puzzles hard enough to be worth tackling and familiar enough to be entertaining. And this book wouldn't be complete without thanking the team behind the decision to establish Vox crosswords in the first place: Susannah Locke, Steven Belser, and Sarah Bishop Woods.

Happy solving!

—Elizabeth Crane
Vox puzzle editor

ACROSS

1 Tenth grader, for short
5 Genre of Tyler, the Creator
8 Less alternative, as a fact
10 Major supporters of the ACA: Abbr.
11 Messing of "Will & Grace"
12 Spectacled Disney dwarf
13 With 18-Across, method of tracking a contagion by using known human interactions (historically made less effective if there is, say, too much community spread caused by big maskless rallies)
15 iPhone assistant
17 Aphrodite's love child
18 See 13-Across
20 Like some footage
21 For grown-ups, but not necessarily naughty

24 Georgia's capital: Abbr.
25 Lists of options at the top of screens
26 Positive word that goes with affirmative actions
27 Initials on invitations

DOWN

1 Norm: Abbr.
2 Valuable mineral
3 Journeys from one bar to another
4 Like Wonder Woman
5 Speed readers used by police officers
6 Gas brand that merged with BP
7 Formal accords
9 Sought a seat in the Senate, say
14 Chicken ___ (popular toddler fare)
15 Lost animal
16 Ticked off about racial inequality, for example
19 Netflix show "___ a Killer"
22 Adore, informally
23 Recipe measure: Abbr.

by Patrick Blindauer

ACROSS

1 Tiny trail blazers
5 "___-daisy!"
9 One who might take you for a ride
10 Zoom site
11 Safe shake
13 "Betty Boop" bit
14 Maker of the Beefy-T
15 Better words?
17 Cooper and Gaga's "___ Is Born"
19 Citizen of a virtual sandbox
22 Four-dimensional continuum
24 Scrabble piece
25 Inside forces
26 Pens in, say
27 Symbol called a key of the 2-Down

DOWN

1 Baldwin of "30 Rock"
2 See 27-Across
3 Kitchen conversation
4 "Hamilton" letters
5 In the city
6 Hashtag, in a past life
7 Less than most
8 Pumps (up)
12 Maurice Sendak's "___ the Wild Things Are"
16 Medieval clubs
17 Italian wine region
18 Cycle after rinse
20 "All good!"
21 Interlock
23 Good gossip, in drag slang

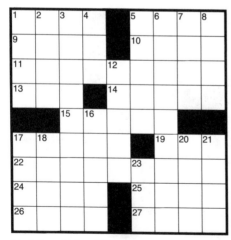

by Juliana Tringali Golden

ACROSS

1 "A Pep Talk in Every Drop" brand
6 Sugar maple tree product
9 Artist's stand
10 Cubes in a drink
11 CeeLo Green's "Forget You," e.g.
13 Showtime dramedy starring Mary-Louise Parker
14 There are 52 in the Gregorian calendar
16 Genre of classical music
18 Bird referenced in describing a great burden ... or an epic golfing feat
23 Burglarize
24 Key hit when starting a new paragraph
25 Where hogs go wild
26 Off to the ___

DOWN

1 Gender identity pronoun
2 Roadside assistance group: Abbr.
3 1960s psychedelic acronym
4 Floral neckwear
5 One can make a dinner date run long
6 Cornbread and coleslaw, most times
7 Substance registering between 0 and 6 on the pH scale
8 Many have their own Instagram accounts
12 "Good heavens!! A mouse!!!!"
14 Annual award for online excellence
15 Significant time period in history
16 Rowboat requisites
17 Movie storyline
19 Messenger material, in biology
20 Not needing a prescription: Abbr.
21 Word that ironically comes immediately after the refrain of the nursery rhyme "Three Blind Mice"
22 Twelfth graders: Abbr.

by Adesina O. Koiki

ACROSS

1 "Darn!"
5 Observers of the High Holy Days
9 Indian royal
10 Belgian ___ (pet that's technically a rabbit)
11 "This is just too much"
13 Relevant
14 Pub offering
15 Sense that something's up
21 Montmartre residents, e.g.
22 "Parks and Recreation" co-star Ansari
23 Voyeurism, e.g.
24 Russo of "Velvet Buzzsaw"
25 Lucille Clifton's "homage to my hips" and similar poems

DOWN

1 Make like an icicle
2 Electoral contest
3 Letting in a slight draft, maybe
4 Entice
5 R&B singer behind the album "Chilombo"
6 Spot for an icicle
7 Tiny songbird
8 Gmail folder with a paper airplane icon
12 Apt rhyme for "bills"
15 Practice for a boxing match
16 Ikea store, stereotypically
17 Environmental activist Brockovich
18 Work like gangbusters?
19 "___ With an E" (show based on a Lucy Maud Montgomery book)
20 Sounds of disapproval

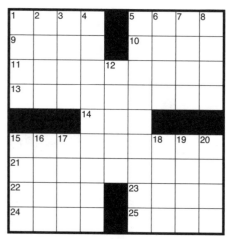

by Will Nediger

ACROSS

1 Concern for a fiscal conservative
5 Tennis match units
9 Mosque leader
10 Sequence of events in a novel or film
11 Comic musician Neil who released the mashup album "Mouth Dreams" in 2020
13 Animal with large antlers
14 "Last but not ___ ..."
15 Option in a smartphone's clock app
17 Chicago's busiest airport
19 Religious woman dressed in a habit
22 Workout routine involving many air punches
24 Clive who was cast as Bill Clinton in the miniseries "Impeachment: American Crime Story"
25 Nullify
26 "What ___ is new?"
27 "Manhattan Beach" novelist Jennifer

DOWN

1 Yahtzee players roll them
2 Name that's a citrus fruit in reverse
3 Payments after an audit, maybe
4 Initialism to an oversharer
5 Shopping free-for-all
6 Online classes and such
7 Fancy word for "clothing"
8 "Right now!"
12 He tried to catch Bugs
16 Title character for Renee Zellweger in a 2000 comedy
17 Instrument aptly featured in Bo Burnham's song "Oh Bo"
18 Werewolf's sound
20 Steak-grading American agency: Abbr.
21 Like some bright colors
23 Prompt for an actor

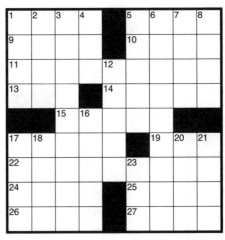

by Andrew J. Ries

ACROSS

1 2010 health legislation, in brief
4 Sorta
9 "Cupid is a knavish ___": "A Midsummer Night's Dream"
10 "What ___ to say is ..."
11 It's by your side
12 "Toy Story" character
13 With 20-Across, early election option
15 ___ von Bismarck (namesake of North Dakota's capital)
16 Brainstorm result, hopefully
20 See 13-Across
22 Recorded for later viewing
25 Lovelace of early computing
26 Responsibility
27 When repeated, sound of eating
28 Backsplash stuff
29 Mother on a field trip, maybe

DOWN

1 Memorable Texas mission
2 Unit equal to 200 milligrams
3 Come clean about
4 Fuzzy fruit with a golden variety that is SO GOOD
5 "Consider it done!"
6 "The Matrix" hero
7 Steven Tyler, to Liv
8 Some unspecified number
14 Plea from a needy boyfriend, perhaps
17 Shelley's "Cheers" role
18 Establish, as a scholarship
19 Athlete's peak performance
21 Horatian creations
22 Nostalgic hashtag for a certain weekday
23 Comedian Wong
24 Bud

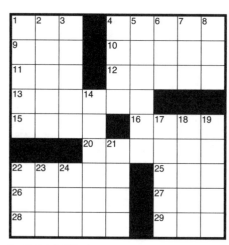

by Patrick Blindauer

ACROSS

1 "Finding Your Roots" airer
4 Negative vote
7 "___ we having fun yet?"
8 It's all part of the act
10 Roman goddess of peace
11 Tricky tactics
12 Headache helper
14 Hard seltzer that inspired a slushie craze on TikTok
17 One-named "Connecting" actress who was the first trans person to star in a network sitcom
18 Loved (on)
20 Step in a side hustle?
21 Super stars
22 Health ins. option
23 Website with many restaurant reviews
24 Top number?

DOWN

1 Fleshy tropical fruit
2 Cheeky
3 Sid Vicious or Johnny Rotten, in a band
4 Glow on the Strip
5 Not none
6 Positive response
8 Bagel toppers
9 Mouse action
13 What's served at the Genius Bar
15 Moving manga
16 Word before train or after station
18 Like many craft projects, for short
19 Sappho's "___ to Aphrodite"

by Juliana Tringali Golden

ACROSS

1 Us or People, briefly

4 Back talk

7 Grammy winner for the album "Shepherd Moons"

9 Like feet in a yoga class

10 Pitching legend and World Series champion who passed away in August 2020

12 ___ Rose (Guns N' Roses frontman)

13 First name in Disney villainy

17 Nickname of 10-Across, with "the"

19 German luxury car

20 Juneteenth activist Lee (who was a guest at the 2021 ceremony in which it officially became a federal holiday)

21 Fit of irritation

22 Beefeater products

23 Possible end to an MMA contest: Abbr.

24 Actor Daniel ___ Kim

DOWN

1 What 10-Across was for 12 years of his Hall of Fame career

2 Span between enero y diciembre

3 Site where many New Year's resolutions begin in earnest

4 London washroom

5 Boiling hot state

6 For every

8 Together

9 Selfish teammate

11 Corporate VIP

13 Southern hip-hop subgenre

14 ___ Raheem ("Do the Right Thing" character)

15 Fatty substance, to a chemist

16 Yogi's pose

17 Word before asleep or casual

18 "Anything ___?"

by Adesina O. Koiki

ACROSS

1 Some partners, casually
4 Target for a train robber
8 With 5-Down, scholar who coined the term "intersectionality"
9 Hatchet
10 Like Tom Jones and Catherine Zeta-Jones
12 Voice actor Strong
14 Formal "Don't look at me!"
15 Medical procedure that might find a fracture
17 Conflicted kind of relationship
18 United Arab ___
19 Sounded like a cow

DOWN

1 Place for Scrabble or Battleship
2 Little white lie
3 Bumped off, as a dragon
4 Like cake batter, hopefully
5 Surname that appropriately intersects with 8-Across
6 Earmark
7 Phrased in a different way
8 Kit ___ bar
11 Jazz piano master Earl
13 Blacksmith's surface
16 Eliel Saarinen's son

by Will Nediger

ACROSS

1 It might be at the end of the line
5 Slightly open
9 Pay for a hand
10 Coke : South :: ___ : Northeast
11 One standing out in their field?
13 Product that may be derived from coal
14 Trip around the block, perhaps
15 Figure in many religious jokes
18 Physical figure, for short
19 "The ___ Mutants" (2020 superhero film)
21 Business with mud baths and mineral springs, maybe
24 Utah ski resort
25 Oktoberfest offering
26 Level
27 Part of YOLO

DOWN

1 Observe Ramadan
2 Members of a pre-Columbian civilization
3 Important day for a recent hire
4 "Could've Been" singer
5 Wide silk tie
6 2020 Libertarian presidential nominee Jo
7 Fuss or foofaraw
8 Far from experienced
12 Xbox button
16 Like the Arctic
17 Stave off
20 Careful
21 Derby, for one
22 Horror filmmaker Roth
23 "Euphoria" network

by Andrew J. Ries

ACROSS

1 Badgers
5 Recedes, as the tide
9 Bassoon's baby brother
10 Ingredient in some smoothies (no, not ACAI)
11 With 23-Across, CEO of 15-Across
12 Show to a chair
13 Fluorescent bulb alternative, for short
14 Salamandridae family members
15 Electric car company since 2003
17 Common wedding gift
19 "Uncle, this is a Montague, our ___": "Romeo and Juliet"
22 It may be stolen
23 See 11-Across
24 "Excuse me"
25 Setting for most of "Cast Away"
26 Like an overly curious person
27 Bus. drivers: Abbr.

DOWN

1 Coward knighted by Queen Elizabeth in 1970
2 Code word for "A"
3 Happy days
4 Obama, once: Abbr.
5 Supporter of the arts?
6 Lost power, perhaps
7 Gravy holder
8 Filming locations
14 "Snowden" org.
16 The Joker, to Batman
17 Jackie of "Rush Hour"
18 Jovial sounds
20 Munch Museum setting
21 ___ out a victory (barely wins)
23 Word before check or drop

by Patrick Blindauer

ACROSS

1 One who commits to a party
7 Remain calm
10 Slow-moving arboreal creature
11 My fellow Americans'
12 Create a falsehood
13 End of a line
15 Wee, to a Scot
16 Fall fliers
18 "If I'm wrong, I'll eat my ___!"
19 Shows derision for, nasally
21 Gratin cheese
22 Tiptoes

DOWN

1 Bread that comes in light, dark, and pumpernickel
2 Mercedes-Benz ___ AMG
3 Stereo dial: Abbr.
4 Pocket calculator?
5 Rough measures
6 Zap in the microwave
7 Baby bringers of folklore
8 Restoring accuracy to
9 Bubble makers
14 It's on again
17 Eye affliction
20 Beach body?

DIAGONAL

3 Commit to a party?

by Juliana Tringali Golden

ACROSS

1 Pictures, drawings, and the like
4 Vigor partner
7 Seafood, on a dinner menu special
9 Sic bo necessity
10 When doubled, an exclamation of agreement
11 Like some eBay items
12 Astronomical path
14 "The Galloping ___" (nickname of football legend Red Grange)
15 Bias
16 It might be seen through a whiteout
17 Distinguishing Bette Davis feature, highlighted in a 1981 tune
21 Pound hound sound
22 IPA ingredient?
23 Eve of "Killing Eve," e.g.
24 Trail ___

DOWN

1 Wood from which many baseball bats are made
2 Blanche portrayer on "The Golden Girls"
3 ___-la-la
4 Drop in on
5 Body Count frontman
6 ___ school
8 Trendy hairstyle modeled from a classic punk look
9 Rave rhythms
13 Weasley of the Harry Potter books
14 1989 film that won Denzel Washington an Oscar
15 Bass guitar playing technique
16 "The Trouble With Maggie Cole" airer
18 Root vegetable in African dishes
19 Old Testament high priest
20 "On the Basis of ___" (2018 RBG biopic)

by Adesina O. Koiki

17

ACROSS

1 Birds in a V
6 Hoops players
8 With only a few spots left
10 Taylor Swift song inspired by "Romeo and Juliet"
11 Legal org.
12 Middle of a pickleball court
13 Fancy containers
15 "Oh my!"
16 Denial in Deutsch
17 Acronymic "If you ask me ..."
18 Tea brand once owned by Starbucks
19 Williamson of the Pelicans
20 Distort, as data
21 Doesn't just sit there

DOWN

1 Light a fire under
2 "___ Fanning's Fan Fantasy" (2017 short)
3 Yale students
4 Delivered
5 Like comfort-maximizing keyboards
6 Number one priority at work?
7 Annie Oakley, for one
8 Shows off ostentatiously
9 Constricting snakes
14 Winter fall
15 Great Pyramid site

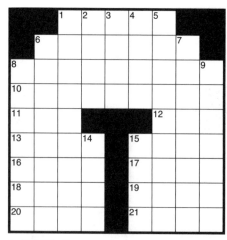

by Will Nediger

18

ACROSS

1 Collected
5 Organization that includes the Power Five conferences: Abbr.
9 "The Man" singer Blacc
10 Units in physics class
11 ___ harina (corn tortilla flour)
12 Ones with a hive mentality?
13 Act of unintentional personal embarrassment
15 Leopard print features
16 Device subject to some driving restrictions
20 Certain circus performer
21 Eponymous bourbon distiller Williams
22 Portentous occurrence
23 Study books
24 Saturate
25 Some clinic workers: Abbr.

DOWN

1 Zoom chat need, for short
2 "Sad to say ..."
3 Don't go out at night?
4 Regimen that might be designed by a nutritionist
5 "Happy to help!"
6 Ruminates on
7 Prayer conclusion, maybe
8 Brayer
14 Quaint term for "metrosexual"
16 Money-minded execs: Abbr.
17 Muppet who rapped the alphabet
18 Tandoor-cooked bread
19 Wraps up

by Andrew J. Ries

ACROSS

1 Network with an eye for a logo
4 Like some horse-and-buggy riders
9 It's got a long arm, they say
10 "Queen of Salsa" ___ Cruz
11 ___-Wan Kenobi ("Star Wars" role)
12 Titan who holds up the world
13 With 20-Across, meatless grilling option
15 "Frozen" sister
16 Iolani Palace setting
20 See 13-Across
22 Safe
25 Component of many science courses
26 On the ocean
27 "The Young and the Restless" actress Longoria
28 Thing that will keep your toy from running away
29 Highest Scrabble letter value

DOWN

1 Flower bud used to flavor some cigarettes
2 Biblical tower location
3 Hearty drinks
4 Berry often found in a bowl
5 Shower participant?
6 Under the weather
7 "Chandelier" singer
8 Experiences, as doubts
14 Features of Gothic roofs
17 End of a shoelace
18 Ho's companion
19 Like some planning
21 State whose highest elevation is at Kings Peak
22 Kilmer of "Real Genius"
23 Had wings, say
24 Letters on postage stamps

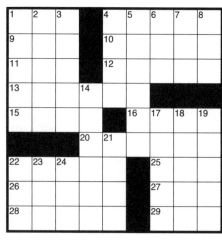

by Patrick Blindauer

20

ACROSS

1 Sailor's mop
5 Many pals
9 Hotel, India, Juliett, ___
10 "Consider it done"
11 Civil rights activist Baker
12 Gumbo ingredient
13 "___, but okay" ("That's a strange thing to brag about ...")
15 Photoshop producer
16 Like "The Queen's Gambit" or "Watchmen"
20 Killer whale
21 Clear accessory?
22 Regard as
23 Pine (for)
24 Latin "to be"
25 Resist a hit, in Reno

DOWN

1 Distort, as a fact
2 Cunning
3 Mutual savings?
4 Sorry!, e.g.
5 Buffoons
6 Low-cut fall footwear
7 Old Italian bread?
8 Soul label whose name evokes piles of records
14 A deer! A female deer
16 Foreshadow
17 Red states?
18 Moon goddess
19 Avant-garde

by Juliana Tringali Golden

ACROSS

1 ___ Ketchum ("Pokémon" protagonist)
4 Corn eater's refuse
7 "Full Frontal" host
8 Bluff response
10 Italian-bred mastiff
12 Stereotypical pirate feature
13 "This is a library! Be quiet!"
15 Uno, in Ulm
16 Stone to cast?
18 Term describing the climax of numerous 2011 Denver Broncos games
22 "Treatment" for a jellyfish sting in a "Friends" episode
23 Livestreaming bane
24 "True ___!" (slangy agreement)
25 Frat house delivery, on many occasions

DOWN

1 1970 hit by the Jackson 5
2 Black or Red, for example
3 Blue ___ (state bird of Delaware)
4 U.S. soccer legend Lloyd
5 Daily Planet photojournalist
6 WordPress creation
8 Treatment for swelling
9 Well-argued
11 Last name of sisters in the film industry
13 "Princess of Power" of cartoons
14 Tendency
16 Small earring
17 To be in arrears
19 Kind
20 Astronaut Jemison
21 Meatloaf ingredient

by Adesina O. Koiki

ACROSS

1 Need for a cross-country trip?
5 Pond layer
9 ___ screen (phone feature)
10 FX show about the ballroom scene
11 Instrument that sounds like a duck
12 City in 23-Across
13 Push-up product developed in Canada
15 "___ Maria"
16 German "Delightful!"
22 Imitated
23 The Hawkeye State
24 Worshiped one
25 "Star Trek" villains with a hive mind
26 Indication to leave a message
27 Terrier named for an island

DOWN

1 Like rush hour traffic
2 E-reader whose name is an anagram of 19-Down
3 Worshiped one
4 Hightail it
5 Dish that might require a lot of napkins
6 Search thoroughly
7 Password enterer
8 Butte relative
14 "Tambourine" rapper
16 "Hold up!"
17 Prom style, often
18 Light gas in lights
19 "The Story of a New Name" or "We Need New Names"
20 Out of whack
21 Fury

by Will Nediger

ACROSS

1 Thyme pieces
7 Talented up-and-comers
9 Snakes that make a loud noise
11 "Empire" co-star Nicole ___ Parker
12 Frequent ___
14 Prefix with second and technology
16 Unofficial mascot of Stanford University
17 Squash or pumpkin, for example
19 Onetime division of the IRS: Abbr.
20 Result of eating ice cream, for some
22 ___ film ("Friday the 13th," e.g.)
23 Go around

DOWN

1 Leapt
2 Ruler in ancient Egypt
3 Groups following celebrities?
4 "Pick," in football: Abbr.
5 Letter between Foxtrot and Hotel in the NATO phonetic alphabet
6 Refine, as ore
8 Mu daet diao condiment
10 Boils with anger
13 Alludes (to)
15 Brand with a Smart Clean line of toothbrushes
18 When the Normandy landings occurred during World War II
21 Venomous biter

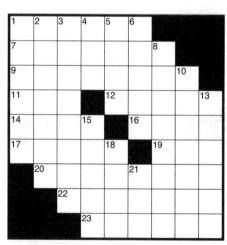

by Andrew J. Ries

ACROSS

1 "Raiders of the Lost Ark" serpents
5 "Your zipper's down"
9 It's just one of those things
10 Well-___ (wealthy)
11 Prefix with -poly
12 Brand in the freezer section
13 With 20-Across, place where your vote actually matters in the U.S., thanks to the Electoral College
15 ___ Majesty
16 Draw to a close
18 Stole
20 See 13-Across
23 Chain with links?
25 Shape of a certain D.C. office
26 "Don't let the ___ hit ya where the good Lord split ya!"
27 They've got talent
28 "Jeez Louise"
29 Arm : elbow :: leg : ___

DOWN

1 Bread boxes?
2 Put on the air
3 2002 Jodie Foster film
4 Jagger, for one
5 Bolted down some nuts, say
6 Blissful state, in slang
7 The ___ (U2 guitarist)
8 Tie up, as a boat
14 Sequoia fluid
17 Everglades bird
18 Supposedly common dog name even though I've never met one
19 "Gulp"
21 Strip at the end of a sprint
22 If-then-___ statement (programming device)
24 Dig for some dirt

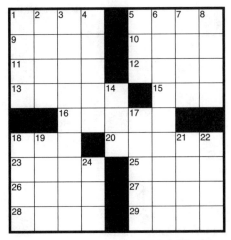

by Patrick Blindauer

ACROSS

1 Clandestine USSR group
4 U.K. lavatories
7 Rude expression
9 Ruffle
10 Come out on top
12 Forum greeting
13 Zoom VIP
14 Honey brew
16 It can be hot or not
18 Talk like a Real Housewife after too many Pinot Grigios
20 Clandestine U.S. group
21 "Sleep well!"
23 Dog with a wrinkly face
24 Plays by oneself?
25 Big mess
26 Bring in

DOWN

1 2019 whodunit starring Daniel Craig and Ana de Armas
2 Line-drawing study?
3 "Not on a ___!"
4 Panoramic lens
5 Dangerous paintball opponent
6 Sun spot?
7 Dog-paddled, perhaps
8 Baseball scorecard letters
11 Office phone add-on: Abbr.
15 Firework that doesn't work
17 Digs in
19 OR pros
21 Rte. finder
22 + or – particle

by Juliana Tringali Golden

ACROSS

1 "12 Days of Christmas" milkers
6 Gym staple
8 Epic failure
10 Small stretch
11 Tributary of the Rio Grande
13 Prank message written on a dirty or snow-covered car
14 Multipurpose utensil
17 Mary Ann Evans, ___ George Eliot
18 "Disturbia" performer, to fans
19 Tide turned?
20 Bills rarely dispensed by ATMs
21 They might be connected by children or detectives
22 Trike rider
23 ___-Ida

DOWN

1 2002 Africa Cup of Nations soccer tournament host
2 ___ League (22-nation group)
3 Watson company
4 Alternative medicine advocate Chopra
5 Fruits of the blackthorn
6 No. 1 compadre
7 Mexican pro wrestler
9 Hall of Fame golfer who won the 1992 U.S. Open
12 Adjustable car parts
13 "It's all in the ___"
14 Like venues at 18-Across shows, probably: Abbr.
15 Ben & Jerry's quantity
16 Cookie with a "Thins" variety
19 Tokyo, once

by Adesina O. Koiki

ACROSS

1 10 Downing Street?
7 Title for Christ
9 Flower in a song from "The Sound of Music"
12 Clumsy oaf
13 Drink that was once safer than water
15 Fashion show fiasco
16 Houston or Jackson
20 "The Heartbreak Kid" director
23 Provide a voice-over for, maybe
24 Renters' agreements

DOWN

1 Edgar Allan ___
2 Birth control option like Mirena
3 Piece of equipment at a French bistro
4 Penne ___ vodka
5 Serving of cereal
6 Cookies and cream cookie
8 Creations for many school projects
10 Do a certain winter sport
11 Juice from a tree
13 Bonobo, e.g.
14 Reaction to a funny bit
17 You might be told not to touch it
18 Concerning, on a memo
19 Fashion designer Wang
21 Chowed down
22 "Gladly!"

by Will Nediger

ACROSS

1 Instrument dubbed the "brass bass"
5 Put away
9 Katy Perry program, briefly
10 Opera performance
11 Analytics-based sports philosophy, and the name of a Brad Pitt film
13 Wrap up
14 ___ & Young (accounting giant)
15 Performers that may wear berets
17 Rude push
19 Tam som cuisine
22 Tampa Bay Rays manager, aptly named due to his 11-Across approach
24 Scary-sounding lake
25 Tiny bit
26 Gardener's unwanted growth
27 Buck

DOWN

1 Smartphone display
2 Soup noodle
3 One of several on Craig's list?
4 "Pale" or "sour" beverage
5 Fencer's blade
6 Adapt for a foreign audience
7 Lubricates
8 Poet Whitman
12 Gulf of Aden nation
16 Covered with vines
17 Distort, as data
18 "Take this"
20 Starting on
21 "Goodness gracious!"
23 Rogue

by Andrew J. Ries

ACROSS

1 Like winters in Chicago
6 Rx order
9 Top caste member in "Brave New World"
10 The "cruellest month," according to Eliot: Abbr.
11 With 20-Across, what the people of Maryland and Missouri voted for by proposition in 2022
13 Hand down, as a verdict
14 Sound of astonishment
17 Detective's undertaking
18 Verdict challenge
20 See 11-Across
24 Brand at the laundromat
25 "The Black ___" (first season of a Rowan Atkinson show)
26 Major mess
27 Adjust, as a watch

DOWN

1 Prince ___ of Shakespeare, or ___ Prince of Broadway
2 Hoppy quaff
3 Dungeons & Dragons, e.g.: Abbr.
4 Chinese dog breed
5 Hearty partner
6 Protege producer
7 Props for "Hamlet"
8 Rapper-producer who is not actually a physician
12 Make feel like a part of the group
14 War and H-O-R-S-E, for two
15 Socially distant
16 Floral arrangement
19 Not shut all the way
21 Pop-ups, probably
22 Wedding announcement word
23 Three-man play about a completely white canvas

by Patrick Blindauer

30

ACROSS

1 "Fleabag" network
4 Request divine intervention
8 Tic-tac-toe win
9 Producer Witherspoon
10 Agitated espresso drink
12 "You gotta believe me!"
13 Nasdaq competitor, with "the"
14 Ancel-cay, say
16 Gold holder
18 Readied the bow
21 Sick of staying in (but not actually sick, so that's good)
23 Oatmeal brew
24 "Black-ish" dad
25 Sound feature
26 Sound feature?

DOWN

1 Role on "Below Deck": abbr.
2 ___ chic (artsy style)
3 Building bloc
4 WPM center
5 Prefab
6 Regarding
7 "Ouch!"
9 Play out, as a scene on "Drunk History"
11 Cereal with the updated slogan "Kid-tested. Parent-approved."
15 What skateboarders try to catch
16 Whispered alert
17 Springfield bus driver
19 Klein who co-founded Vox.com
20 Colorist
22 Co-star of Betty, Bea, and Estelle

by Juliana Tringali Golden

ACROSS

1 Org. with Trail Blazers, Cavaliers, and Mavericks
4 Track a beat, perhaps
7 Chest muscles, for short
9 Apple or reactor part
10 Fall back (on)
11 Angers affirmatives?
12 It can allow a lot of light in
14 Acorn-bearing tree
15 It can allow a lot of light in
20 One of a sinful septet
21 Military outfit
23 Restrict the flow of
24 Stint in office
25 A third of the Holy Trinity
26 "Just a ___!"

DOWN

1 Home of Tiny Desk Concerts
2 Euphemism used when having "the Talk"
3 Org. co-founded by Jane Addams
4 Duration of most soaps
5 Gout-causing acid
6 Work well together
8 Kicks for fun, e.g.
9 Common summer holiday sighting
13 ___ for the course
15 Quagmire
16 Cognizant about
17 "The Great British Bake Off" necessity
18 They are prevalent in binary code
19 Don't shout it in a crowded theater
22 Run ___ (Bay Area nickname of a high-scoring 1-Across trio from 1989 to 1991)

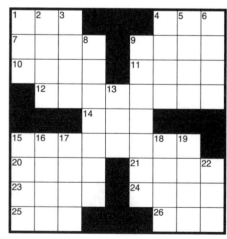

by Adesina O. Koiki

ACROSS

1 Array in an ashtray
6 Never-before-seen NFL point total
10 Do a perfunctory job
11 Features in many beach selfies
12 Discovery
13 Card in a royal flush
14 Wish you could undo
15 Icelandic yogurt
17 Wind-powered plaything
18 Made more sympathetic
20 Releases early
21 Sources of eyes for witches' brews

DOWN

1 Phantom threat
2 Vessels in Thomas Browne's "Hydriotaphia"
3 Result that's not allowed in tennis
4 End-of-the-week initialism
5 Takes on, as Stella Gibbons or Joseph Heller would
6 Striking impression
7 Annual event for many
8 Notes from a meeting
9 "Quite so"
16 Like albino alligators
17 Highland dress item
19 "Both Sides, ___" (Joni Mitchell song)

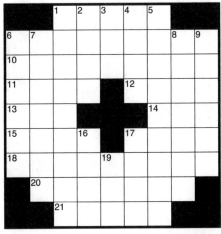

by Will Nediger

33

ACROSS

1 Item in a distillery
4 Tokyo-based automaker
9 Alternative to a .college domain
10 Mayhem
11 References for checking one's priors
13 Company with a noteworthy 2020 launch
14 Use a laser beam, perhaps
15 Grimy stuff
19 In ___ (together)
21 First state to adopt an official state question ("Red or green?")
24 Zodiac ram
25 Part of NSFW
26 Olympic figure skating event
27 Road trip expense

DOWN

1 Segment of song lyrics
2 Change with the times
3 "Life Goes On" rapper
4 Throbbing pain
5 Gardetto's competitor
6 Its president is Sheikh Mohammed: Abbr.
7 Degenerate
8 "Kick-___" (2010 superhero film)
12 Amy who is a distant cousin of a U.S. senator
16 Putting into service
17 Drink topped with marshmallows, maybe
18 Speed units at sea
20 Mitchell & ___ (sportswear company)
21 Brief time out
22 Series of years
23 Gaming debut of 2006

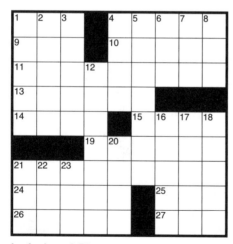

by Andrew J. Ries

ACROSS

1 Ending with wear or tear
5 BBQ leftover
8 Pittsburgh-based food company
10 Place to get a little rest and relaxation
11 Supplement
12 Margarita glass rim stuff, in Mexico
13 Poet Browning
15 Fashion accessories of 2020
18 Big name in makeup
19 Feeling of fury
20 "___ Suite" (Neil Simon play)
24 O'Hare posting: Abbr.
25 Like some bears
26 Actor Waterston
27 It's put on by a wrapper

DOWN

1 "Bingo!"
2 King or queen?
3 Pot top
4 Menu selection
5 They may be kissed or kicked
6 ___ plug
7 Calls a stop to
9 Portable version of a popular video conferencing program
14 Primary concern?
15 "Lord of the ___"
16 Big supply line
17 Old Eric Clapton band
21 Cookbook words
22 Give a quick spin in the kitchen, say
23 "What ___ YOU lookin' at?"

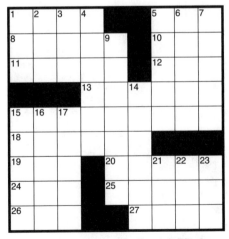

by Patrick Blindauer

ACROSS

1 Admit (to)
4 Gallivants
9 "WALL-E" companion
10 Iconic riff in "Sweet Child o' Mine"
11 Hot weather formation
13 Out of body?
14 Lets go of woe
19 Step-by-step guide
20 Cold weather formation
24 "WALL-E" company
25 Frightened expression?
26 "Humble" dwelling
27 Busy spots for RNs

DOWN

1 Closet wood
2 Pistil round
3 Dough in a Mexican bakery
4 Communal commute
5 Gender-neutral pronoun
6 Beach buggy, briefly
7 Look inside?
8 Norse sun goddess
12 Boom maker
15 It's made of many millennia
16 "Shucks"
17 Direct action
18 Custard ingredients
20 Relaxation location
21 Bit of cacao
22 Palindromic kitchenware brand
23 Bunch of bills, bills, and more bills

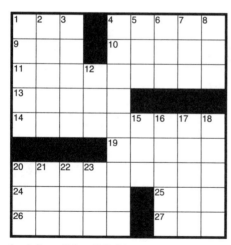

by Juliana Tringali Golden

ACROSS

1 Message broadcast to police cars: Abbr.
4 Longtime Saints quarterback Drew
6 Famous misspelling of 1992
8 Saint, in Portuguese
9 "... ___ and none, and ___ just left town."
11 Paints a word picture of
14 Earlier
15 Financial advisor Suze
16 Socrates' P
17 "Right away, boss!"
19 It was upgraded from an asteroid to a dwarf planet in 2006
20 Utters, in slang

DOWN

1 Gallery items
2 Vegetable from a pod
3 They are placed inside casinos
4 Voice amplifier that is normally away from view, for short
5 Classic Stanislaw Lem sci-fi novel
6 Two kings, perhaps
7 Figure etched by skaters
8 ___-mo
10 Barnyard sound
12 Identifies
13 Boring sound?
18 ___ Percé (indigenous people of the American Northwest)

by Adesina O. Koiki

ACROSS

1 Cry to an annoying sibling
5 South Korean filmmaker ___ Sang-soo
9 The floor, in a kids' game
10 Someone you look up to
11 "Ploughing in the Nivernais" animals
12 Competitive advantage
13 Jeanette who wrote "Oranges Are Not the Only Fruit"
15 Fertilized cells
16 "Bleak House" protagonist Esther
22 South American berry
23 ___ seeds (egg replacement)
24 Compact in design
25 What a stumped solver might ask for
26 Yard or garage event
27 Talks on and on and on

DOWN

1 Snail-like
2 Vehicle with a meter
3 Device that might be self-cleaning
4 Silent art form
5 Pecking order
6 "What are the ___?"
7 Scrapped, as a mission
8 Low land in the Highlands
14 Night before a holiday
16 Talk back to
17 Kelly Lytle Hernández's sch.
18 Fan letters, e.g.
19 Sect for the majority of Iraqis
20 Sound from a sty
21 Team with which Juan Soto won the World Series, casually

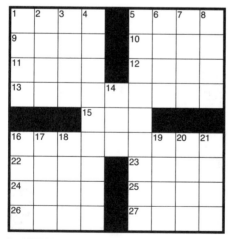

by Will Nediger

ACROSS

1 Degrees held by many CEOs: Abbr.

5 Word in a famous Neil Armstrong quote

9 The younger of the Avett Brothers

10 Wheel rod

11 Fruit that would be apt to eat at a party

13 Unit of a spreadsheet

14 [Face with tears of joy emoji]

15 Service provided at some gyms

17 Org. with a Free File program

18 Doherty who played Princess Anne on "The Crown"

19 Particles that may be created through beta decay

22 Keto diet no-no, for short

23 Tab on many a restaurant's website

24 Versified tributes

25 Lead-in to school or cook

DOWN

1 Bouillon cube additive: Abbr.

2 Book best consumed while basking, say

3 In one's free time

4 "We ___ Overcome"

5 Track revolution

6 Piece of informative journalism

7 Choice that leaves no in-between option

8 Jordan who co-created "The Last O.G."

12 Tree related to the birch

15 Dos + tres

16 Create a wavy pattern in

20 "The Last O.G." channel

21 "How ya doin'?"

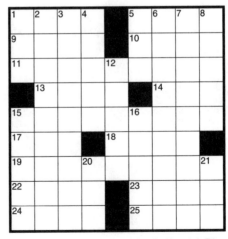

by Andrew J. Ries

39

ACROSS

1 Plane's cousin
6 Fisticuffs
9 Font similar to Helvetica
10 Cotton gin inventor Whitney
11 With 4-Down, site of the 1941 attack that led to the U.S. entering WWII
12 Part of the Rolling Stones logo
13 Word for an unruly child
15 State whose motto is "With God, all things are possible"
18 Cut loose
19 Revise, as map boundaries
21 Length of a history book chapter
22 Country that attacked 11-Across/4-Down
26 Wonder-full sound?
27 Path that sounds like a future-tense contraction
28 ___-Cat (off-road vehicle)
29 Religious ceremonies

DOWN

1 Something you stand to lose?
2 "Chances ___"
3 Spanish family member
4 See 11-Across
5 Palindromic publication
6 "Take it easy!"
7 Fruit used in Greek cuisine
8 Completely exhausted, in slang
14 Home to Honolulu, where 11-Across/4-Down is located
15 They may be Golden or Fudge-Dipped
16 Wading bird in the board game Wingspan
17 Territory in which Mount Rushmore sculptor Gutzon Borglum was born
20 Cracked
23 Winter clock setting in L.A.
24 "For God's sake, a pot of small ___": "The Taming of the Shrew"
25 Platform on which I spent many hours playing "Zelda" and "Contra"

by Patrick Blindauer

ACROSS

1 Athletics club?
4 More cordial
6 Diminutive dessert
8 "Don't you worry 'bout a thing"
10 Healthy and happy
11 Equal opportunity?
12 Spices up
13 Artery opener
14 Language suffix

DOWN

1 Demographer's data point
2 Some Oscar nominees
3 Game of garbled messages
4 Bad beings
5 Self-___ (standing on one's own)
6 Blackfin and bluefin
7 Sleeveless tops
8 Peanut butter brand whose logo is almost the same upside down
9 Classic Jag

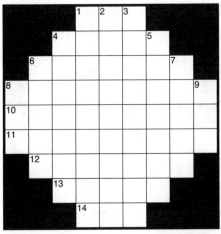

by Juliana Tringali Golden

ACROSS

1 Groups of items in an auction
5 Yosemite ___
8 Approximately
10 Towel possessive
11 Popular payment app
12 "Shut ... up!", in textspeak
13 Homophone of 29-Across
14 Crew team's needs
16 "Inside the NBA" cable channel
17 Horror movie franchise beginning in 2004
20 One might be right or obtuse
23 "Modern Family" actress Winter
25 Battery size in many TV remotes
26 Music genre with "death" and "speed" varieties
27 Colleagues of RNs
28 Direction not seen in any U.S. state name
29 Homophone of 13-Across

DOWN

1 ___ cake (dessert with molten chocolate)
2 Comply with, as orders
3 Color hue
4 Total of numbers added
5 Putts, chips, bunker shots, and the like, on the links
6 Squad goals
7 Big Apple arena: Abbr.
9 Nickname of Dallas Cowboys legend Ed Jones, listed at 6-foot-9
15 1990s Texas governor Richards
17 "Ditto!"
18 Word before code or 51
19 Basic human intelligence
21 ___ Jaye ("G.I. Joe" sergeant)
22 Abate
24 "___ Pray Love" (2010 Julia Roberts film)

by Adesina O. Koiki

ACROSS

1 Arcade game with arrows, briefly
4 The ___ (Canada's men's curling championship)
6 Stranded, as a whale
8 Chance to see your online friends in person
10 Tiny bug
11 Dialect in which "be" can describe a habitual action, for short
12 Situation that could easily turn ugly
14 Tool used with a hammer
15 Country on the Arabian Peninsula
16 Turf

DOWN

1 "You'll laugh, you'll cry" movies
2 Craps cubes
3 Overly polished, maybe
4 Road around a city
5 Captured back
6 Film composer Jon
7 It might be filled with down
8 Troublemaking tyke
9 A square one doesn't fit in a round hole
13 Ticklish toy

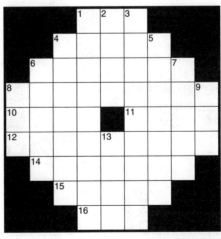

by Will Nediger

ACROSS

1 Wolf's cries
6 Light ___ feather
9 Best-case scenario
10 Spot for a napkin
11 Does a preliminary wedding planning step
13 Streaming service launched in May 2020 (and renamed in May 2023)
14 Worn-down pencil
16 "___ to the World" (Christmas song)
17 Piano recital performance
19 Identifying implant for a pet
23 The Beavers of the Pac-12: Abbr.
24 What "naked" barbecue lacks
25 Acquire
26 Rhyming antonym of "cheap"

DOWN

1 "The Horse and ___ Boy" (novel set in Narnia)
2 Poem of praise
3 Like Seattle's climate
4 Salon that specializes in extensions
5 Hunk of granite
6 Major attraction in San Antonio
7 Skewered meat dish
8 Highest point
12 Singer who won a Grammy with SZA for their 2021 hit "Kiss Me More"
14 Bad music, derisively
15 Like the title gems in a 2019 Adam Sandler film
17 Haze of pollution
18 Lightly throw
20 Shade of color
21 Hockey rink surface
22 Vim and vigor

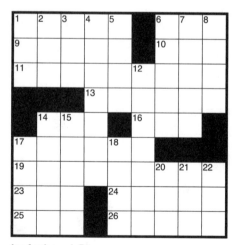

by Andrew J. Ries

ACROSS

1 "Dang!"
5 Gmail folder
9 "That hurts!"
10 Ingredient in some wet wipes
11 Certain circus creature
12 Previously owned
13 With 16-Across, another name for Hanukkah
15 Focus of three Nobel Prizes: Abbr.
16 See 13-Across
21 iPhone speaker, say
22 Armstrong in the book "First Man"
23 "Frozen" character who likes warm hugs
24 Twistable treat
25 Computer storage unit
26 Tree house

DOWN

1 Tip, as one's hat
2 The Golden ___
3 Bullets, in card slang
4 1966 hit for Frank Sinatra
5 ___ blanc (French grape)
6 "Frozen" character who knows how to "Let It Go"
7 Christmas, in carols
8 Hall of Famer Williams
14 French for 18-Down
16 Like fried chicken, perhaps
17 Where to find a band of brothers
18 English for 14-Down
19 Musical markings that connect notes
20 Opening at the casino
21 Have a bawl?

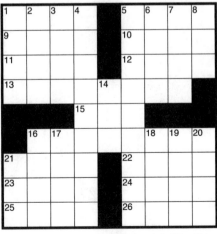

by Patrick Blindauer

ACROSS

1 Good eats
5 Home to Zion National Park
9 Sharpen, as a skill
10 Lil Wayne's "___ Lisa"
11 Length × width, for a rectangle
12 Norse trickster god
13 One who precipitates prosperity
15 Author Bellow
16 Grand hotel?
19 Water form
22 Moment for speedy spending
24 Letters that are not in sync
25 Moving-day rental
26 Peek in the medicine cabinet
27 Last word in a puzzle, for instance

DOWN

1 Scorch slightly
2 Festive circle dance
3 The Shirelles' "Dedicated to the ___ Love"
4 Moves on to baby food
5 German marks
6 Went on sabbatical, maybe
7 Tennis great Huber
8 Stuff in a beehive
14 Blend of two or more things, such as Christmas and Hanukkah
16 Advanced degrees for creative folks
17 Narrow valley
18 Month after abril
20 Rickman who played Severus Snape
21 Heal
23 Phillipa of "Hamilton"

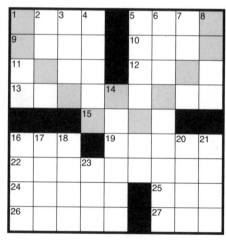

by Juliana Tringali Golden

46

ACROSS

1 D&D, for example: Abbr.
4 Units of a molecule
9 Antonym of "'neath"
10 "Exactly!"
11 Star of the 1978 movie "The Wiz"
13 Forward part of a plane
14 Nickname that appears on the official football used during NFL games
18 Splashy affair
20 "Black Jeopardy!" show, in brief
21 Tehran is its capital
22 Seldom-used pronoun (unless you're a stickler for grammar, of course)
23 Act like a shark, in a way
24 Congregation's benches
25 Root beer brand name
26 ___ Norris (Hogwarts feline)

DOWN

1 Retina cell near a cone
2 Shar-___
3 Onetime ESPN sports/pop culture blog named after a legendary early 20th-century sportswriter
4 Degrade
5 Sick partner?
6 Plastic ___ Band (post-Beatles group)
7 Musical counterparts to Booker T., with "the"
8 "Help!" letters
12 "Look Ma" follower
15 Court official
16 Is sure about
17 Their "slippery" versions have been used for medicinal purposes
18 ___ the lily
19 Pi, for a circle with a radius of 1
22 Typing stat still seen on some résumés: Abbr.

by Adesina O. Koiki

ACROSS

1 Sign of an impending shark attack
4 Research team
7 Cards with one pip
9 Showed up
10 Rough-skinned ___ (toxic salamander)
11 Instrument for Elaine Douvas
12 Reception room, in Canada
14 Activity with climbing and jumping
15 Hole where five strokes is a bogey
16 Butter alternative
17 Lorde song with the lyric "it feels so scary getting old"
20 Group between boomers and millennials
21 "Streak" or "chat" intro
22 Abbr. for an album of movie music
23 LGBTQ part

DOWN

1 Season tickets holder, maybe
2 Substance on the Moon
3 One not getting much sleep
4 Working in Alberta's oil sands, e.g.
5 Comédie romantique subject
6 Lambic or lager
8 Nintendo series about animals in space
9 Red and white, for the Canadian flag
13 "Citizen Kane" studio
14 ___ in comparison (isn't nearly as good)
15 Jump up and down at a punk rock show
18 "Babe" sound
19 Recon figure

by Will Nediger

ACROSS

1 Like half of the digits
4 Christmas fare
7 Low digits
9 Flavor of many cat treats
10 They process tax returns
12 Buildings at the base of snowy slopes
13 Hole-punching tool
14 Some log-in information
20 Extra-long dress
21 "___ the date" (wedding invitation preceder)
22 Earnest request
23 Former name of Thailand
24 Splinter group
25 Hotel chain that's also a prefix meaning "everything"

DOWN

1 "Respect" writer Redding
2 Dweeb
3 From the Indian subcontinent
4 Like an indecisive jury
5 Card night payment
6 The "m" in the formula $E = mc^2$
8 Class of workers not paid hourly
9 Sitcom starring Jason Sudeikis as a soccer coach
11 Graduation day garb
14 They call balls and strikes, for short
15 Black Friday event
16 Corporate bigwig, briefly
17 Seriously injure
18 Spiegel who co-created Snapchat
19 Highway hauler

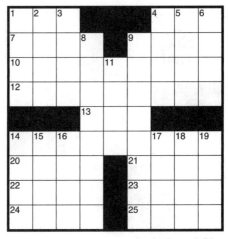

by Andrew J. Ries

ACROSS

1 Thing on a list
5 Gardner of "Mogambo"
8 Emphasis word after yes or no
10 Setting for "Young Frankenstein"
11 With 15-Across, holiday greeting
12 This, that, or the other
13 Comes to know
15 See 11-Across
18 They may be grand
19 "_ucy in the _ky With _iamonds"
20 "... five golden ___ ..." ("The 12 Days of 15-Across" lyric)
24 Bob Hope's entertainment group: Abbr.
25 Setting for "Antony and Cleopatra"
26 Antonym's opposite: Abbr.
27 Former NPR host Conan

DOWN

1 Suffix with social or cynic
2 Equal, in a way
3 Be human, according to a saying
4 "Camelot" character
5 Bedside table device
6 She always has a White 15-Across
7 Fathomless chasm
9 Scenic spoiler
14 Part of many addresses
15 A little above average
16 ___ fit (tantrum that my daughter throws if I sing the wrong words to any song from "Frozen," God forbid)
17 Poisonous gas that's the product of uranium decay
21 Host of the 2010s web series "Emoji Science"
22 Fig. on a transcript
23 Home of the World Chess Hall of Fame: Abbr.

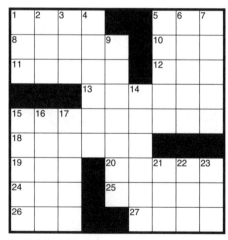

by Patrick Blindauer

ACROSS

1 Approves, quickly
4 It was finally ratified by VA in 2020
7 Problematic subject
9 Indie folk band Bon ___
10 Something from everyone
12 Parsley and bulgur salad
13 Tax pro: Abbr.
14 Shows off
18 Windup wingding
20 "Oh sugar, I spilled the sugar!"
21 Candy company with a Nuts & Chews box
22 Canadian expanses: Abbr.
23 Web coding format

DOWN

1 "I'm, like, shocked"
2 Mario conveyance
3 Greek colonnade
4 Not for good
5 Loan mod.
6 "___ is a line around your thoughts": Gustav Klimt
8 Wheel wear
9 León lizards
11 Temporary restaurant
14 Of
15 Where baby books are read
16 Glam band named for a dinosaur
17 Prominent poppy part
18 Kai phat khing cooker
19 Designer initials

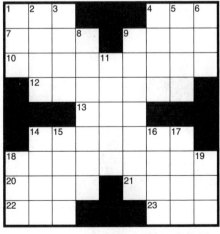

by Juliana Tringali Golden

ACROSS

1 "___ Christmas" (Donny Hathaway)
5 Olive of comic strips
8 Prefix denoting "all"
9 Egg ___ young
10 "___ Christmastime" (Paul McCartney)
13 French fry seasoning?
14 "Christmas in ___" (Run-DMC)
17 Possible response from a child if told Santa Claus is not real
19 Insane way to run
21 Executive's aide: Abbr.
22 Easternmost point of the Silk Road
23 College entry exam
24 How a boxing match may end
25 "All I Want for Christmas Is My ___ Front Teeth" (various, including the Chipmunks)
26 Opposite of NNE

DOWN

1 Service provided by AAA
2 Medical coverage group
3 Overnight trip stop
4 PBS's "Science Kid"
5 What presents left under the Christmas tree are considered before Christmas morning, perhaps
6 "All I Want for Christmas Is ___" (Mariah Carey)
7 What Santa's guffaw would look like in textspeak
11 Course for a U.S. immigrant: Abbr.
12 "Take it easy!"
14 Must
15 Food scrap
16 Drenches
17 "___ Christmas" (Wham!)
18 "___ Mommy Kissing Santa Claus" (various, including the Ronettes and the Jackson 5)
20 "Do They ___ It's Christmas?" (Band Aid)

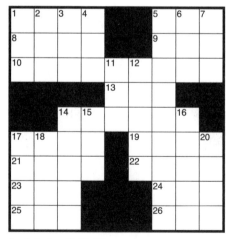

by Adesina O. Koiki

ACROSS

1 Unpleasantly moist
5 Non-binary person, casually
9 Slothful species in "The Time Machine"
10 Apt rhyme for "crocodile"
11 With 14- and 19-Across, punchline of a joke about a clown
13 Nearest the center
14 See 11-Across
15 Genre for O-Town or Aly & AJ
19 See 11-Across
21 Model Hadid
22 Pick up Hanukkah gifts, e.g.
23 Tons
24 Singer Mercedes or swinger Sammy

DOWN

1 VIP at a ball
2 Former student, briefly
3 "Me? Impossible!"
4 Texts for tots
5 Include
6 Minor things to pick
7 Rorschach test picture
8 "___ out!" (ump's cry)
12 Muscat resident, e.g.
15 Something to pin on the donkey
16 Brand with cinnamon toast waffles
17 Spanish "eight"
18 Common condition whose first two letters stand for "polycystic"
19 ___ Tour
20 Bitter beer style

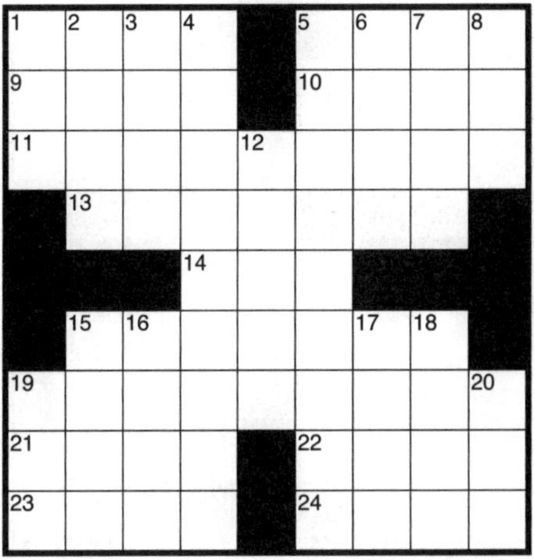

by Will Nediger

ACROSS

1 Progressive spokeswoman
4 Closest confidante, for short
7 Losers of the Miracle on Ice game: Abbr.
9 "FBI" co-star Ward
10 Tip for a marketer
12 With 14-Across, some Christmas gifts
13 Edge of a glass
14 See 12-Across
19 Tournament game preceding the championship
20 Breathe heavily
21 Rating for shows not suitable for kids
22 Poetry and pottery and such
23 Puppy's high-pitched bark

DOWN

1 Complain
2 Hurdle for an aspiring attorney: Abbr.
3 Home of the Nobel Peace Center
4 "It's ___ real!"
5 Flapper on a pole
6 Short-lived phenomenon
8 New enlistee
9 Like skinny jeans
11 Small flat-bottomed boat
14 Char, as on a grill
15 2007 superhero movie featuring Leonardo, Michelangelo, Donatello, and Raphael
16 Sin that sounds like Nevada's postal abbreviation
17 Malek of "Mr. Robot"
18 ___ on the wrist (light punishment)
19 Workplace for a massage therapist, maybe

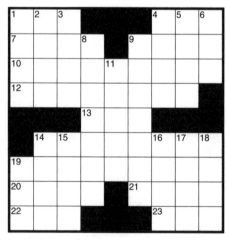

by Andrew J. Ries

54

ACROSS

1 With 5-Across, company that the 14-Down is suing for allegedly breaking antitrust laws

5 See 1-Across

9 Bread in Bologna, once

10 Harmless, as threats

11 Salutes with feet?

12 Basketball Hall of Famer Jason

13 Establishes a new meaning for

15 Railroad stop: Abbr.

16 Tricksters?

22 Computer science pioneer Turing

23 "Star ___"

24 Going ___ (bickering)

25 Neutrogena alternative

26 With 27-Across, what 1-/5-Across is accused of becoming

27 See 26-Across

DOWN

1 Carpet tile company, or a bloom in Bilbao

2 Classroom helper

3 Rep

4 Enters gradually

5 Part of a two-piece suit

6 One-eyed Norse deity

7 Barq's Famous ___ Tyme Root Beer

8 Shoe brand since 1916

14 Org. suing 1-/5-Across

16 Word of respect

17 A cappella group member

18 Forward movement, in football

19 Guthrie who performed at Woodstock

20 Name that sounds like a way to peacefully protest police brutality

21 Grey Goose alternative

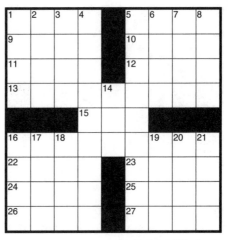

by Patrick Blindauer

ACROSS

1 Ingredient in a Hawaiian slider
5 ___ facto
9 Preppy brand coveted by the Lo Life Crew in 1980s New York
10 Biblical ark type?
11 Tools that punch holes in leather
12 2019 romance "Queen & ___"
13 Troublemaker
15 One or more
16 Begin again
18 Tsp. or tbsp.
19 Make trouble
21 Little dog pursued by Almira Gulch
23 Move, quickly
24 Where buns are done
25 Bit of Shakespeare
26 Less than one
27 Psyche's love

DOWN

1 Prepare for battle
2 Sitting at the head of the table, perhaps
3 "Fixed it"
4 Grandma of folk art
5 Shut-___ (people who stay home during a worldwide pandemic, e.g.)
6 Animal called "God's dog" in Lapland
7 Patron of sailors and abdominal pain
8 "I didn't expect that"
14 USPS delivery
17 Eagle's perch
18 The whole syllabary
20 Tosses
22 "Give Peace a Chance" collaborator

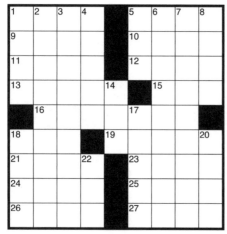

by Juliana Tringali Golden

ACROSS

1 With 28-Across, a new beginning
6 Victoria's Secret item
9 Influential French rabbi of the 11th century
10 ___ al-Fitr (end-of-Ramadan feast)
11 Recovering from an injury
13 "O Sole ___"
14 Queries
15 Identify, say
18 Cautious way to think
20 NYC art museum, with "the"
23 Sports broadcaster's exclamation upon seeing a great netminding feat
25 Charged atom
26 Garnishes for gimlets
27 "Illmatic" rapper
28 See 1-Across

DOWN

1 Email header line
2 Hindu royal
3 Tallinn residents
4 "Tone it down!"
5 Make a run for it, archaically
6 Hive residents
7 Indoor ice skating locale
8 Stirs into the pot
12 West of old movies
16 Perform a role
17 ___ on Wheels America
18 Bed size smaller than a full
19 "Mind. Blown!"
20 "Dear ___" (1995 Tupac Shakur hit)
21 Word attached to what or how
22 Cause of student stress
24 Enjoy a La-Z-Boy

by Adesina O. Koiki

ACROSS

1 AC number
4 YouTube ad option
8 ___ Stoppable (Kim Possible's best friend)
9 Places for strikes and spares
11 Before, in verse
12 Scientist Joliot-Curie
13 Sinus doc
14 John in the Mercury Seven
15 First woman to win the Pritzker Architecture Prize
17 Decree
18 ___ mode
19 Sport invented in Italy
20 With 21-Across, holiday on which, for instance, '20 might lead into '21
21 See 20-Across
22 "Sex Education" star Butterfield
23 Part of a crib
24 Park Jae-sang's stage name

DOWN

1 Move past easily
2 Storm chasers' quarries
3 Just not right
4 Not in the ___
5 Camila Cabello's real first name
6 "The couch beckons!"
7 Broke
10 Dismiss
16 Capital of Ghana

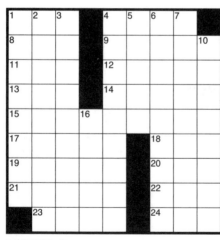

by Will Nediger

ACROSS

1 Off-the-wall
6 One of many on a hotel rack
9 Poet Lorde
10 Blinding rage
11 "Welcome!"
13 Completely lose it
14 "Not only that, but ..."
17 Extractions that often end in -ite
18 Rodent kept as a companion
20 Another name for blackjack
24 It might be bald-faced
25 "That's a ___" (eel-themed parody version of a Dean Martin song)
26 Big letters in haute couture
27 Sudden upward rise

DOWN

1 Annoying audio/video mismatch
2 "___ Kind of Traitor" (2010 John le Carré novel)
3 Artistic tribute
4 Like hand-me-down clothing
5 Beast of Himalayan lore
6 Lesser in degree
7 Verbally spar
8 Termites and cockroaches, perhaps
12 "Consider it taken care of"
14 In a fitting way
15 "Fire Under My Feet" singer Leona
16 Metal associated with Pittsburgh
19 Boxes often marked with dollar signs
21 Hockey great Bobby
22 Ragged racehorse
23 Retina's organ

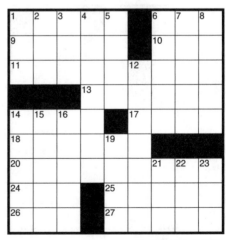

by Andrew J. Ries

ACROSS

1 What knocking may mean
6 Dance like Savion Glover, though probably not nearly as well
9 Drive in Beverly Hills
10 Famous Skull Island resident, for one
11 15-Across divided by 20-Across
12 "I'm cold!"
13 Dome-ciles?
15 11-Across times 20-Across
18 Comic's opposite
19 Poetic preposition
20 15-Across divided by 11-Across
24 Buddy
25 Got off the ground, in a way
26 Sarah's sweetie in "Guys and Dolls"
27 Start of a counting rhyme

DOWN

1 Org. with filing deadlines
2 Edgar Allan who wrote "The Gold-Bug"
3 -ly word, usually: Abbr.
4 Believing, they say
5 "Auld Lang Syne," for example
6 Prohibited practice
7 Front part of a stage
8 Latin for "in itself"
14 Chinese fruit in the soapberry family
15 Corvette roof types
16 ___ havoc (unleash mayhem)
17 Not late
21 Akira Kurosawa film based on "King Lear"
22 Prefix with Pen
23 Printemps follower

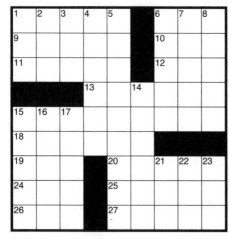

by Patrick Blindauer

ACROSS

1 New Orleans player
6 Flowering
8 Seemingly impossible event, figuratively
10 Muhammad who said, "Don't count the days, make the days count"
11 401(k) alternative
12 Pulitzer-winning novel by Donna Tartt, with "The"
16 Circular edge
17 French vodka brand
23 Smooth over, say
24 Synthetic
25 One with a Ouija board, perhaps
26 Worry

DOWN

1 Shell dweller
2 Starting line?
3 Kind
4 Negative responses
5 In it ___ it (focused on victory)
6 Book art, in editor-speak
7 Designer Jacobs
8 "Mixed" metaphor
9 "Nope, I'm good"
13 Launderland apparatus
14 Fruit in buccellati
15 Parting words
17 Navigation initials
18 Issa of "The Lovebirds"
19 Night before
20 Shell propeller
21 Take to court
22 Office phone line: Abbr.

by Juliana Tringali Golden

ACROSS

1 Daffy rival
5 Stir-frying aid
8 Top floor?
10 Nickname of the 34th president of the United States
11 Acronym of a 1994 commerce agreement replaced in 2020
12 Frito-___ (snack food company)
13 "Yellowjackets" network: Abbr.
14 Form of address said to a baroness
16 It can lead to trouble when it's hot
17 ___ Wednesday
20 Desktop computer brand
22 Group of businesses owned by the same company
24 Cool, '80s-style
26 "Nothing ___!"
27 Word before cell or spell
28 Sheets that 1-Across might appear on
29 Observe

DOWN

1 Prohibits
2 Jazz locale?
3 "You can't be serious!" in textspeak
4 "Take a load off!"
5 Designations of seven Super Bowl champions, most recently the 2020 Tampa Bay Buccaneers
6 Give the thumbs-up to
7 Pivotal
9 Like a positive influence
15 Objective
17 "Back in Black" band
18 Oxford, for example
19 Painful precipitation
21 The middle initial of ACA and ICU
23 Connections, informally
25 Disguise one's roots, in a way

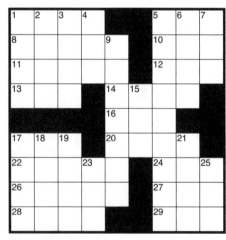

by Adesina O. Koiki

ACROSS

1 Device with a driver
4 Features of many students' anxiety dreams
9 Gotham FC athlete Krieger
10 The Little Mermaid
11 Part of an okra plant
12 With 13-Across, "Normal People" author
13 See 12-Across
15 Uncertain
16 Put together film scenes
20 With 28-Across, "Ordinary People" author
22 Burstyn or Barkin
25 "Not so!"
26 "The Teflon Don" John
27 Shade provider
28 See 20-Across
29 Turn red, maybe

DOWN

1 ___ pants
2 Not engaged
3 No longer saddled by
4 Lack of hardships
5 Saw right through?
6 Need some TLC
7 First name of two Spice Girls
8 On the ___ (inapt anagram of "honestly")
14 NFL team in MetLife Stadium
17 Didn't just eat ramen on the couch
18 Pizza place?
19 Za'atar herb
21 Gram or amp
22 Something laid by a platypus
23 Cindy ___ Who
24 4G ___

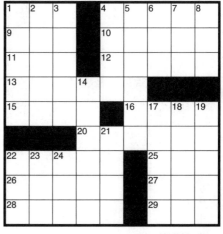

by Will Nediger

ACROSS

1 As a result
5 Skin blemish
8 Food delivery service that held an IPO in 2020
10 Subtly portray
12 Flip over
13 Food delivery service with a flying bike in its logo
17 "Over the moon" or "on cloud nine," for instance
18 "Scarlet" flower in the title of a famous play
23 Food delivery service that's a spinoff of a rideshare giant
24 In a rage
25 Country named after its namesake lake

DOWN

1 URL ending for a college website
2 Burgundy played by Will Ferrell
3 What "Allah" literally translates to
4 Mined material
5 "Jazz From Hell" musician Frank
6 Small refuge in the sea
7 Scottish lord
9 One who keeps the beat
11 Three-foot measures: Abbr.
13 Dot on a domino
14 Hatred
15 Voice role for Donald Glover in 2019's "The Lion King"
16 Had some cocktails
19 Parks partner, for short
20 "I'll pass"
21 Texter's "when will you be ready?"
22 Cause of a trip

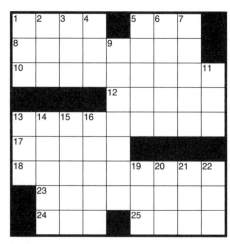

by Andrew J. Ries

ACROSS

1 "Cogito, ergo ___" ("I think, therefore I am")
4 Grasps
9 Water bottle confiscator: Abbr.
10 Actors' Equity, for one
11 Hallow follower
12 *Carpentry tool, and one of six answers that reads the same forward and backward*
13 *Repetitive sound of admonishment*
15 Joints that rejuvenate
16 Big galoots
20 *Co-star of Hanks in "Splash"*
22 *Longtime Honda model*
25 Gershwin brother who isn't George
26 Love so much that one gives an 11 out of 10, say

27 Texter's "I can't believe this is happening"
28 Forbidden activities
29 Spear head?

DOWN

1 *Leaves in, in a way*
2 Consume, as resources
3 ___ ray
4 Alternative to Netflix
5 2,000 pounds
6 "___ and Maddie" (Disney Channel show)
7 Anonymizing surname

8 Source of ads for Baby Spanx and the Love Toilet
14 It may be shot from a cannon
17 Herb with licorice-flavored seeds
18 Where workers wet their plants
19 *Former Iranian monarchs*
21 Leaders in suits
22 Heel
23 "Hey, Hey, What Can ___" (Led Zeppelin song)
24 Part of some German surnames

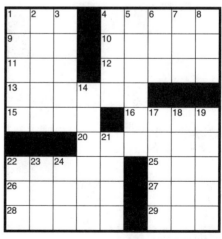

by Patrick Blindauer

ACROSS

1 Woodworking tool
4 National Poetry Month
9 Not post-
10 Momentary slip
11 Hang on
13 ___ voice (reasonable volume at which to speak)
14 Letter opener?
15 Clodhoppers
19 Soften, as sound
21 Bust out
24 Senseless
25 Fixated condition, briefly
26 Supermarket conveyances
27 Place to catch a cumulonimbus

DOWN

1 Rose bug
2 It takes photos on the fly
3 Legendary Nintendo princess
4 Cher or Sade
5 Find a partner
6 It may be led by a dungeon master: Abbr.
7 Kinda-sorta suffix
8 "___ It Be" (last Beatles album)
12 Unlikely to erupt
16 Natural dos
17 Tiny dot
18 Like an everything bagel, or Times Square in the '70s
20 Luau strings
21 Maker of the Cristal ballpoint pen
22 Base runner?
23 It can be lent or bent

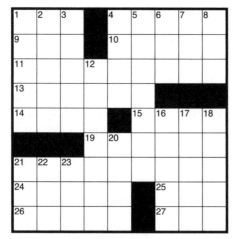

by Juliana Tringali Golden

ACROSS

1 They are essential in doing the twist or playing Twister
5 Navigation letters
8 Product of a brainstorm
9 Home to Timbuktu
10 Of the finest quality
12 Ceremonial dance in Maori culture
13 "Beowulf" and Virgil's "Aeneid"
15 Part of a bride's outfit
17 Reach one's nadir
22 Comply with, as orders
23 Rolls, Jag, or Caddy
24 Spiritual practice of some Buddhists
25 Sketched

DOWN

1 Website visit
2 Marriage pledge
3 European soccer coaching legend ___ Guardiola
4 Melancholy
5 Stares open-mouthed
6 Emotional request
7 ___ Mix-a-Lot ("Baby Got Back" singer)
9 NCAA-affiliated league that includes Manhattan College and Niagara University: Abbr.
11 African pachyderm
13 Consumed, in a way
14 Feeling of sorrow
15 Stage name of one of the members of the Grammy-winning R&B trio TLC
16 Courtroom garb
18 Word repeated four times in a 1963 Spencer Tracy film title
19 Possessive for a couple
20 Native of the Beehive State
21 Tugboat job

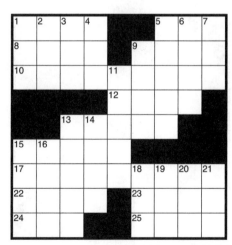

by Adesina O. Koiki

ACROSS

1 Vamooses
8 Oxford college named for an earl
9 Small spicy sphere
10 Absolutely legendary
11 "Wednesday" actress Catherine ___-Jones
12 Oscillate wildly
16 Workers on a set
18 Something to pick up on
21 Union leader?
22 Quality of some dry humor

DOWN

1 Stupefy
2 Odor from a gym bag, e.g.
3 "Broad City" co-creator Jacobson
4 First sets of wheels, for many
5 Gift that pacifies
6 Eisenhower's nickname
7 Darjeeling, for instance
8 Dueler's step
9 ___ Khalifa
13 Whales with matrilineal pods
14 "Minari" star Steven

15 Have debts
17 Risk lung illness, perhaps
18 Risk a thumb prick, perhaps
19 Preceder of "bodies" and "selves" in a classic book on women's health
20 React to a weepie

by Will Nediger

ACROSS

1 Within the ___ of possibility
6 2018 documentary about a Supreme Court justice
9 Country on the Bay of Bengal
10 Belonging to us
11 Title legionnaire in a P.C. Wren novel
13 TV producer Chaiken
14 Only athlete to play in an MLB All-Star Game and an NFL Pro Bowl
18 Tests that require no writing
19 Like Yosemite Sam, lower body–wise
24 A in French
25 Mexican sandwich
26 Laundry detergent capsule
27 Meander

DOWN

1 Unit of a rack at a barbecue joint
2 Billings-to-Bismarck direction: Abbr.
3 Mathematician Lovelace
4 Lucy of "Elementary"
5 Kits that may include a wand and exploding dice
6 "___ are red ..."
7 "Think again!"
8 Color symbolizing authorization
12 Member of the deer family
14 Come to the surface
15 University of Maine town
16 Talked incessantly
17 Not merely most
20 Understood
21 Sound from a guard dog
22 Boarding pass info: Abbr.
23 Calendar unit

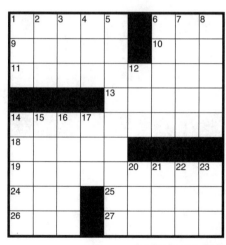

by Andrew J. Ries

ACROSS

1 "Of course!"
4 Where the Platte and Missouri Rivers meet
9 ___ Moulins, Quebec
10 "Treasure Island" captain Billy
11 California baseball team that would probably like this puzzle
13 ___ salts (bath additive)
14 Cousin of "The Addams Family"
15 Beer barrel poker?
17 It's subject to inflation

20 Eternity alternative
24 Bon ami of the Three Musketeers
26 Comparatively friendly
27 Suffix with arch or green
28 "___ of Two Cities"
29 4-Down, initially

DOWN

1 Succulent genus
2 Marjory the Trash ___ ("Fraggle Rock" oracle)
3 Inquires (of)

4 2010 health statute, informally
5 Calendar column: Abbr.
6 Billie Holiday's "Me, Myself, ___"
7 What cold is the absence of
8 Lead-in for prof. or DA
12 "'Salem's ___" (Stephen King book)
16 FedEx delivery: Abbr.
17 Ferber who wrote "Show Boat"
18 Gallop or trot
19 Willy in "Free Willy," for one
21 Eligible for the draft
22 Buster?
23 "Orinoco Flow" singer
25 Monthly expense, for many: Abbr.

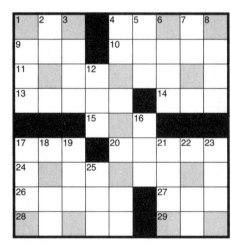

by Patrick Blindauer

ACROSS

1 Auction action
4 One who stands apart?
6 [Knock knock]
8 Endgame maneuvers
10 Jokes like Phyllis Diller's "Housework won't kill you. But then again, why take the chance?"
11 Trademarked stimulant name that's one letter short of the real thing
12 Proves false
13 Dissuade
14 ___ Moines, Iowa

DOWN

1 Made like a dad at a 2 A.M. feeding
2 Soon, very soon
3 Goes off
4 Wielded a light blade?
5 One who likes to unwind?
6 A little time off?
7 Hatcher and Garr
8 Mauna ___, Hawaii
9 9-digit identifier: Abbr.

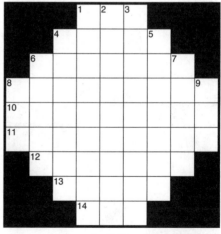

by Juliana Tringali Golden

71

ACROSS

1 Cobb, e.g.
6 Giant American cactus
8 Second opportunity for advancement in a competition, akin to a losers' bracket
10 Slangy affirmative
11 Bitingly funny
12 Multiple Grammy winner whose given first name is Eithne
14 Anterior cruciate ligament location
15 Angle or state lead-in
17 Streamed course
21 Used article given as a partial payment
22 Wray of film
23 Intake suggestion, briefly

DOWN

1 Excessively maudlin
2 99, for Eva Marie Saint in 2023
3 Jean-___ Picard (Sir Patrick Stewart TV role)
4 "That's the spot!"
5 Weary-looking
6 Viewed
7 Scary giant of fairy tales
8 New York city on Long Island Sound ... and a homophone of 11-Across
9 Talent for detail, maybe
13 Cornered
14 Hall of Fame baseball player and longtime New York Mets broadcaster Ralph ___
16 Get ___ of (eliminate)
17 Incredulous interjection, in textspeak
18 Major pitching statistic: Abbr.
19 Humanitatian help
20 "Messenger" or "transfer" genetic material

by Adesina O. Koiki

ACROSS

1 Musical buzzers
7 With 8-Across, raising livestock
8 See 7-Across
11 Love, to Gaël Monfils
12 Maria who was the first Native American prima ballerina
17 Le ___ (French port whose name means "the port")
18 Childbirth-related science
22 Help out
23 Mantras, e.g.

DOWN

1 Capital that's home to the Gardens of Babur
2 Enemy of the state?
3 California wine, casually
4 "If You Leave" band, briefly
5 Paddle
6 Like a fox
8 Beanie or beret
9 ___ Karuna Thurman
10 Fa follower
13 Sword hilts
14 "___ made a huge mistake"
15 Make a huge mistake, maybe
16 "Unbreakable Kimmy Schmidt" co-creator Tina
18 Apple product
19 "... kinda"
20 Political org. with a rose in its logo
21 Emerge victorious

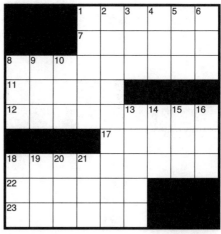

by Will Nediger

ACROSS

1 "ASAP!"
5 Sidewalk edge
9 Preceder of enemy or bishop
10 53-calorie cookie
11 Transports for tour groups, perhaps
13 Course load taken by many first-year college students
14 Actress/singer Graham
15 Countertop cooker with a built-in fan
20 Wood choppers with large blades
22 They're worn at a barbecue joint
23 Russo who played Frigga in the Marvel films
24 The A of TA: Abbr.
25 Mouse trap brand

DOWN

1 "How Do You Sleep?" singer Smith
2 Pre-req for calc
3 Skin issue that affects some cats
4 Make quick decisions
5 Outdoor common area
6 ___ Major (constellation that includes the Big Dipper)
7 Fishing pole device
8 Work supervisor
12 Those who grew one in 1700s Russia had to pay a tax
15 Legendary group in Swedish pop music
16 Eye part that surrounds the pupil
17 Burgles
18 Company higher-up, informally
19 "___ 911!" (sitcom rebooted in 2020)
21 Title for Rick Scott or Tim Scott: Abbr.

by Andrew J. Ries

74

ACROSS

1 Words of wonder
6 Play house?
9 It's connected to the knee bone
10 "Who ___?" (amnesiac's question)
11 Passes over a laser beam, as merchandise
12 Set on fire
13 With 19-Across, first female vice president of the United States of America
15 With 18-Across, 46th male President of the United States of America
18 See 15-Across
19 See 13-Across
21 Morales of "Ozark"
22 Bean that I can't help associating with "The Silence of the Lambs"
26 Musical marking
27 Tablet from Apple
28 Phrase of understanding (not glasses from Apple)
29 Cultivate, as a garden

DOWN

1 Extra play periods: Abbr.
2 Juice box brand with a hyphenated name
3 Org. for heavyweights
4 "Old MacDonald Had a Farm" sound
5 Condiment that's usually horseradish in the U.S.
6 Potato ___
7 Hirsch of "Into the Wild"
8 Giant of industry or mythology
14 Outcast
15 ___ curl
16 Saving graces for the deserted?
17 Wipe out
20 Wedding, for one
23 Swinger at the zoo
24 "Breaking Bad" vehicle
25 Put 2 and 2 together, literally

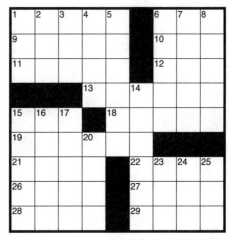

by Patrick Blindauer

ACROSS

1 Impressive ballroom maneuver
4 Dependable person
8 Edible oval
9 Psychic emanation
10 Cat suit?
11 Mad as heck
13 Long (for)
15 Pinot alternative
16 Office abbr.
17 Told tales
18 "___ in the 4-Down" (What a glorious feeling!)
20 Quaint stopover

21 Broken mirrors, e.g.
24 Record
25 Leader of the Pussycats on "Riverdale"
26 Gold meas.
27 Image app

DOWN

1 Thumb one's nose at
2 "Come to think of it, that's probably untrue"
3 Pixar features?
4 See 18-Across
5 Me and my friends'
6 Folly

7 Progressive politician Porter
12 Last word in a fairy tale
14 Star Wars baddie Kylo ___
17 Sour fruta
19 Asian "superfood" berry
20 Kind
22 Minor criticism
23 Where shanties are shared

by Juliana Tringali Golden

ACROSS

1 Flashy, feathery neckwear
4 Chum
7 Washers' contents
9 Gobbled up
10 Proceeding with business
12 Element of a winning hand in blackjack
13 Hemingway's "A Farewell to ___"
14 Comic ___
17 Aspirations
21 Marked by stately beauty
24 Like some medications
25 One may develop into an earworm
26 Crunchy deli sandwich, in brief
27 "Is there something else to that?"

DOWN

1 Switzerland's third-most-populous city and birthplace of Roger Federer
2 Poetic tribute
3 Equine that brays
4 Grouping on Noah's ark
5 It's split during nuclear fission
6 Eye of a camera
7 When doubled, movie title of a 1997 Jim Carrey comedy
8 At some time in the past
11 Least perilous
15 "White Wedding" singer, 1982
16 Before, to a poet
18 Bluish-green color
19 Olivia of "The Newsroom"
20 Number shown in brackets?
21 Indeed.com listing
22 One is seen in the clue to 21-Down
23 Turner who led a slave rebellion

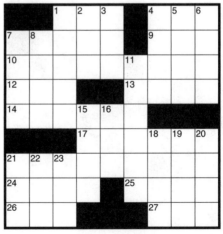

by Adesina O. Koiki

ACROSS

1 Much-mocked Binks
7 Anxiety
8 Rock that's pronounced "nice"
9 Peanut butter brand that, for some, is pronounced the same as "gif"
10 What Meat Loaf won't do for love
14 Portuguese-inspired string instrument, for short
15 Name that's another name backwards
16 Clothing
18 Target of a bowling ball
19 Vampire created by Anne Rice
22 Influential noble family of Italy
23 High-stepping dance

DOWN

1 Poetic onomatopoeia for the sound of a nightingale
2 Golfer Sörenstam
3 Spliff
4 ___ alai
5 Jerk
6 Doctor's order, often
11 Touch-related
12 "POV" singer Grande
13 Cartoon adventurer with a dog named Snowy
17 Alliance of countries
20 Important period in history
21 Closely-guarded ID

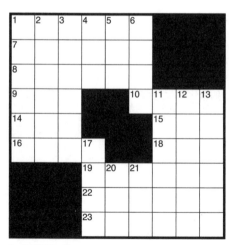

by Will Nediger

78

ACROSS

1 Castle surrounder
5 Not rugged?
9 Display effusive enthusiasm
10 Stench
11 New York Islanders great who holds the NHL record for most consecutive 50-goal seasons (9)
13 Playfully naive
14 Pair worn by a sledder
20 Steeped beverage
21 "Midsommar" director Aster
22 Becomes less strict towards
26 Writer of the bestseller spelled out in this puzzle's shaded squares
27 Individual performances

DOWN

1 Film company whose logo is a roaring lion: Abbr.
2 "That's right, President Macron"
3 Pose a question to
4 "Riverdale" network
5 "Heck yeah!"
6 Elements of some sports uniforms
7 Part of L.A.
8 Opposite of sweet
12 Light punch
14 Sault ___ Marie, Ontario: Abbr.
15 In order
16 Band featuring the Gallagher brothers
17 Backs of necks
18 Ancient city that is the setting of the "Iliad"
19 Lust, envy, or greed, e.g.
23 Brian who launched the record label Opal
24 Khan of Khan Academy
25 Strange sky sight

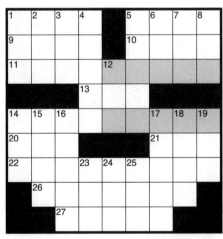

by Andrew J. Ries

ACROSS

1 Balance providers
5 Pad ___
9 Place for plopping or perching
10 Villain who says "I am not what I am"
11 Not done, literally
13 "Cocoon" star Guttenberg
14 Patters at the airport, perhaps
15 Macy's worker, at times
17 Go downhill fast?
20 Sugary snack options
24 Not done, literally
26 Southpaw's pitching arm
27 ___ doctor
28 Pianist born Alicia Cook
29 Nautical rate

DOWN

1 Garage sale words
2 Pup follower?
3 Medieval club
4 Where a kettle may settle
5 "Don't eat yellow snow," for one
6 Word from a watchtower
7 Bronze and Iron, for example
8 Very small amount
12 Midori liqueur flavor
16 Search, as for concealed weapons
17 Put on a pouty face
18 One may be taken before a proposal
19 Uncertain, slangily
21 Place to catch catchers
22 River that starts in Pittsburgh
23 Email folder
25 "___ a Wonderful Life"

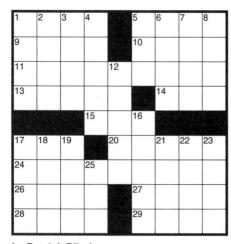

by Patrick Blindauer

80

ACROSS

1 Engrave with acid
5 Not-so-little twinkler
9 Explorer of Nickelodeon
10 Theater opening?
11 "___ Day" (a film about repeat events)
13 Words on either side of a slash
14 "I'm shocked!"
15 Classic Fender guitar, for short
17 Dig in
19 ___ Joe (presidential nickname)
22 "___ Day" (a film about repeat events)
24 ___ speak (right now)
25 "All right, your turn"
26 Refuse to believe
27 Take a breather

DOWN

1 Provocative
2 Rushed (through)
3 City-spanning bus route
4 Act supernaturally
5 In need of good news
6 Bauble at Bubbe's house
7 It's what's the matter
8 Diana of "Game of Thrones"
12 Like smudge-proof mascara
16 Words on either side of a slash
17 "I'm shocked!"
18 Bum
20 Daily journals
21 Awards acronym for Whoopi Goldberg and Viola Davis
23 Quick turnaround

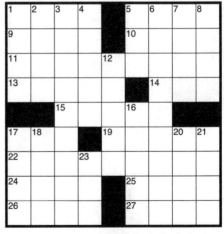

by Juliana Tringali Golden

ACROSS

1 ___ Williams, first Black quarterback to start in, and win, a 15-Across

5 ___ Mahomes, former baseball pro whose son is the only Black quarterback with two 15-Across wins

8 British bottom

9 "Evil Woman" band

10 Satisfies, as a requirement

12 Austrian or Italian peak

13 Party game in which uttering certain words is forbidden

15 Game that, in 2023, featured two Black starting quarterbacks for the first time

19 Lacking + or –, electrically

20 Hall of Famer who was the first Black head coach to win a 15-Across

24 Neither Dem. nor Rep.

25 Native of Warsaw

26 "Duck Hunt" gaming console

27 "Terrible" time in one's life, it is said

DOWN

1 Beaver construction

2 Underground extraction

3 "It's no ___!"

4 Acquire

5 Grammy-winning R&B singer Bryson

6 Grant permission

7 Mononymous Israeli actor who portrayed Tevye in "Fiddler on the Roof"

11 Valued violin, briefly

14 Rudely quick

15 Shiny fabric

16 How the New York Giants finished the 25th 15-Across (Sorry, Buffalo Bills fans!)

17 Small bodies of water

18 Actor Ron who played Tarzan on TV

21 Feminist group founded in 1966: Abbr.

22 Mop & ___ (cleaning brand)

23 "No doubt!"

by Adesina O. Koiki

ACROSS

1 "Ciao!"
8 "I don't think we've been introduced"
11 Color similar to gunmetal
12 Call for help
13 Mystics player Elena Delle ___
14 Texting standard, for short
15 Supplement
18 Admonishment when a surprise party's guest of honor is arriving
21 Basic belief
23 Don't do anything for
24 Geek Squad company

DOWN

1 "The Tunnel" novelist William
2 "I think we're ___ something ..."
3 Glorifying verses
4 Pigment cousin
5 Big risks
6 Zastava autos often considered among the worst cars ever
7 Deserve
9 Was a candidate
10 One of three on a tuatara
14 Anti-apartheid activist Biko
15 Often-injured knee structure: Abbr.
16 Female kangaroo
17 Lackluster
18 Challenging roommate for a neatnik
19 "Little Fires Everywhere" streamer
20 Lamarr who co-invented frequency hopping
22 Take to the stage

by Will Nediger

ACROSS

1 "Strangers with Candy" star Sedaris
4 Work with a needle
7 Fuel for some stoves
9 Kismet
10 Certain waterfront property
12 Fake meat brand popular at Thanksgiving
13 Final part
14 Garments that lack armholes
18 Song traditionally sung by sailors
20 Finger prod
21 Beverage that may be marketed with a bee-inspired name
22 "___ questions?"
23 Crunches work them

DOWN

1 Hole maker
2 A drawbridge may go over one
3 Ono who sang "No, No, No"
4 Meskwaki allies
5 Website with a "Craft Supplies" category
6 Itty-bitty
8 Crowd cheer at a basketball game
9 Bronx neighborhood with a namesake university
11 Intuitive feeling
14 One doing drudge work
15 "Sort of an ___ afterbirth" (wine review from Michael Scott)
16 ___ Day vitamins
17 Synonymous rhyme of "jab"
18 Hot tub
19 Gridiron measurements: Abbr.

by Andrew J. Ries

ACROSS

1 Emhoff who raised some eyebrows at the 2021 inauguration
5 Other people, per Sartre
9 High time?
10 Céline Moinet's instrument
11 Container for leftovers
13 "Bucko"
14 Cone head?
15 Ming who does not make vases, as far as I know
17 "___ Loves You"
20 Spots for studs
24 North Carolina town in aviation history
26 Do some pressing business
27 Site for buying treasures or trash
28 Protagonist Arthur from "The Hitchhiker's Guide to the Galaxy"
29 Say it ain't so

DOWN

1 "All's Well That ___ Well"
2 Skating maneuver
3 Apple for Apple, appropriately
4 Like some birds
5 Tool used when the plot thickens?
6 Recedes, as the tide
7 Word after student or home equity
8 Brand with a Harry Potter line
12 Cartographic "boot"
16 Sounded impressed
17 "___ Row" ("Little Shop of Horrors" song)
18 Bring on board
19 Alma mater of George Orwell and Hugh Laurie
21 Popular pet name
22 Nicole's "Moulin Rouge!" co-star
23 "The ___'s the limit!" (shout to a bartender about the most one is willing to spend on vodka)
25 Letters on red animated sticks

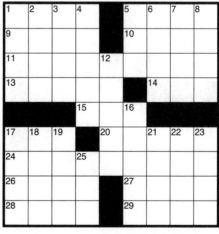

by Patrick Blindauer

ACROSS

1 Software success story of 2020
5 Repeated sound from Beaker on "Muppet Labs Field Test"
9 Personal energy field
10 Kendrick of "A Simple Favor"
11 Kept going in spite of hardship
13 Call to mind
14 Congressman and activist who organized protests for voting rights in 12-Down
18 Poppy product
19 Help someone in need
24 Maple, but not sugar
25 Cupcake decorator
26 Talk back or back talk
27 Like a fresh morning windshield

DOWN

1 [Bzzz]
2 Yours and mine
3 Rock offering
4 More in Mexicali
5 Thandiwe's character on "Westworld"
6 Fund
7 Japanese mushroom
8 Sheets in the window
12 Landmark city in the civil rights movement
14 Shakes up
15 Rock offering
16 Tap dancer Gregory
17 Works in "The Full Body Project"
20 Stowed away
21 One with heart, perhaps?
22 Fresh off the line
23 Light on vermouth

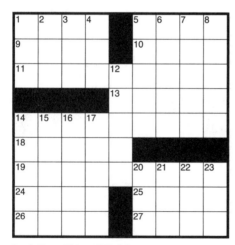

by Juliana Tringali Golden

ACROSS

1 2006 Nintendo release
4 Fork over some lettuce
7 Crafts partner
9 Prosecutor's pursuit
10 They appear at one-yard intervals
12 Succor
13 Geographical region whose name is lent to an NCAA Division-1 conference that contains the USA ... that is, the University of South Alabama, of course!
17 Plant reproduced from spores
18 Beginner, in gamer lingo
20 "Cogito, ___ sum" (Descartes phrase)
21 Common item received on one's 19-Down
22 Like 2022, but not 2023
23 Jazzy James
24 "Thanks for coming to my ___ Talk!"
25 Casual greeting

DOWN

1 "I didn't get my way!"
2 Savings method, familiarly
3 Possessive pronoun
4 Breaking this on a golf course is good
5 Pose a question
6 Word that someone who gets on one knee is hoping to hear
8 "Saturday Night Live" alum Molly
9 Voice inflection
11 Will Smith/ Tommy Lee Jones film series, for short
13 Beginning of every tennis rally
14 Goaded
15 Unwilling
16 Sweet cake that sounds like a crime to eat
17 12-inch lengths
19 Annual milestone, casually

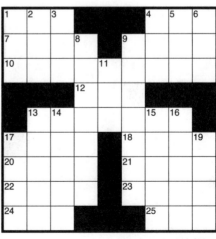

by Adesina O. Koiki

ACROSS

1 Served as a prelude (to)
6 Feed for keeping up with a blog
9 "Lift ___ Voice and Sing"
10 Seventh Greek letter
11 See 3-Down
12 2020 hit for Cardi B and Megan Thee Stallion
13 Tech whose last letter stands for "recognition"
14 Revisions
16 Eye annoyance
18 Pale ___
19 See 15-Down
21 Genre for "Serial" and "Making a Murderer"
25 Welfare, metaphorically
26 Something to comb out
27 Supplement seller

DOWN

1 Bricks in some tiny houses, informally
2 Turn out, as a tenant
3 With 11-Across, sitcom set in Northern Ireland
4 Not online, casually
5 The Big Board: Abbr.
6 Returning an area to its natural state, in conservation
7 The Founding Fathers, for example
8 Drains, as energy
15 With 19-Across, milking workers, quaintly
17 "Nice to ___ you" (greeting in an inbox)
20 Don't just sit there
21 Finger-wagger's sound
22 Tried to catch the bus, maybe
23 Craft in many a conspiracy theory
24 "... plus some other stuff": Abbr.

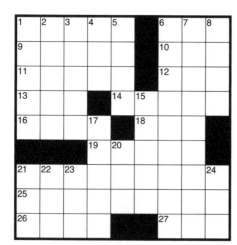

by Will Nediger

ACROSS

1 Transmitted subtly
6 Taxi's scaled-down version
8 "Tool Man" of classic sitcom fame
10 Top ten list ender
11 Three-time Grammy winner Rawls
12 Teensy-weensy, before "bitty"
14 Twenty dispensers
15 Trahan who represents Massachusetts in the U.S. House
16 Team that shares SoFi Stadium with the Chargers
17 Toledo's lake
18 Tennis great Nastase
19 Turquoise-like color
20 Taoism's Lingbao or Quanzhen, for example
21 Tiresome
22 Twisty curve of a road

DOWN

1 Track event that may determine one's starting position
2 Tunnel-building insect
3 "Tenet" organization ... which in real life was once headed by George Tenet: Abbr.
4 Treacherous, like some winter roads
5 Too-good-to-be-true stories
6 Treat with a green creme filling
7 Television crew equipment with retractable poles
8 Target of "training" for a young child
9 Tater type
13 Triangular road sign with a red border
14 Turn up

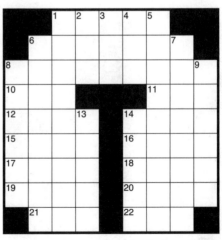

by Andrew J. Ries

ACROSS

1 Malek of "Bohemian Rhapsody"
5 Set of 108 for Uno
9 Tons
10 Kamala's stepdaughter Emhoff who signed with IMG Models
11 ___ Christian Andersen
12 Site where I found a copy of the Cloak & Dagger board game I had as a kid
13 Hammett's detective of fiction
15 "Boo-yah!"
16 Cardinals or Orioles, for example
21 "The Time Machine" race
22 Tiny ___ Galaxies (tabletop game)
24 ___ now (so far)
25 "Toy Story" character with two knobs
26 City that surrounds the Vatican
27 Present, as a problem

DOWN

1 One for the team?
2 "More's the pity!"
3 Lisa of the Louvre
4 2000 single by Bon Jovi
5 Sound slumber
6 Site of Napoleon's first exile
7 Not au naturel
8 Danny of "White Christmas"
14 Moment, for short
16 Animal on California's flag
17 "In addition ..."
18 Weaving contraption
19 "What have you been ___?"
20 Flickers?
23 Guevara who was the original narrator of "Evita"

by Patrick Blindauer

ACROSS

1 Word on many a street sign
5 High top?
9 Greek goddess of light
10 Jordan Peele feature
11 Art rock band ___ Music
12 Wheel connector
13 Compact rentals
14 Meg of "When Harry Met Sally..."
15 It's said to mark the spot
16 Cable car
20 Leopard spots
24 Like a beehive
25 Way out
26 RuPaul, for one
27 Lean (on)
28 TV's warrior princess
29 Black stone

DOWN

1 Word in the new name for Mr. Pibb
2 Chain that serves Cinn-A-Stacks (sometimes)
3 Casting call?
4 The G in PFLAG
5 Off in the distance
6 ___ Stix (powdered candy)
7 Human rights activist Baker
8 Storm and Jubilee, for two
15 It's said to mark the spot
16 Chocolate bar that comes in Left and Right
17 Something to run for
18 Nerve impulse conductor
19 Talkative bird
20 27 × 37 − 999
21 Farm team?
22 Slick
23 Underworld river

by Juliana Tringali Golden

ACROSS

1. "Frontline" network
4. "Fifty Shades of Grey" topic, for short
9. Tree sprouting from an acorn
10. Utters loudly
11. Member of the pioneering '90s hip-hop quartet A Tribe Called Quest known as the "Five-Foot Assassin"
13. "Jack of all trades, master of ___"
14. Borrows for a fee
17. Title bestowed onto Nanak
20. Lagunitas product: Abbr.
22. 1982 George Clinton hit with the lyric "Bow-wow-wow-yippie-yo-yippie-yay"
25. Kind of stove
26. Stockholder's portion
27. "___-Ra: Princess of Power"
28. Becomes gooey

DOWN

1. Breakfast partner of Snap and Crackle
2. "___, humbug!"
3. Potato cover
4. Short movie clip
5. Cosmetics giant Elizabeth ___
6. Actress Long
7. Droplets on the grass at dawn
8. NYC venue nicknamed "the World's Most Famous Arena": Abbr.
12. Place for discussion
15. ___ wave
16. Display
17. Jokes that may be "running"
18. State that hosted the most recent Olympic Games on American soil
19. Went upward
21. Ice and Stone, for two
23. Ending that indicates a belief system
24. Jost's "Weekend Update" co-anchor on "SNL"

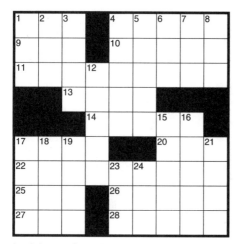

by Adesina O. Koiki

ACROSS

1 "Oh, come on!"
7 Nitpicky people
10 Dermatologist's concern
12 Flute sound?
13 Hashed out
17 Often-misspelled literary middle name
18 Confederacy that includes the Kainai
23 Site of Napoleon's second exile
24 Gradually wore down

DOWN

1 Office-appropriate, briefly
2 "What?"
3 "Washington Black" novelist Edugyan
4 Superlative suffix
5 Cave explorer
6 Cream-filled snack cakes
8 Perfect scores, in some sports
9 Worth heeding
11 Flop
13 Tiny amount of makeup
14 Societal problems
15 Part of a crib
16 Something you might clear online
19 Aptly-named app that tracks your menstrual cycle
20 Ref. work that added "awesomesauce" in 2020
21 United
22 Tiny amount

by Will Nediger

ACROSS

1 Jessica of the "Sin City" movies
5 Gear wheel projections
9 ___ as dishwater
10 Gardener's supply
11 Leave off
12 Questionable, say
13 Flipper's transaction
15 Payments to participate
19 Fatefully happen to
20 "Not to mention ..."
23 James in the Rock and Roll Hall of Fame
24 Millennials, alternately
25 "You gotta be kiddin'!"
26 They're traditionally eaten on Christmas Eve in Italy
27 Campsite digs

DOWN

1 Love, love, love
2 Unit of light brightness
3 Collection of lesser celebs
4 Some service workers
5 TV-influenced phenomenon in which jurors overemphasize the role of forensic evidence
6 Punch-to-the-gut reaction
7 Image acronym with a debated pronunciation
8 Underhanded
14 Substance used to treat pretzels
16 Phrase on an "Alice in Wonderland" cake
17 Role for Taron in 2019's "Rocketman"
18 Point of view
20 It's just a number, per an axiom
21 Jeans brand
22 Kenan Thompson's show, for short

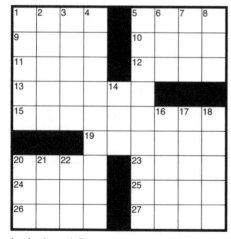

by Andrew J. Ries

ACROSS

1 Capitol Hill helper
5 "The stockings were ___ by the chimney with care ..."
9 Ice ___ (board game with sliding penguins)
10 The Buckeye State
11 Happy hour special, maybe
13 Ted's "Cheers" character
14 One who greets and seats
15 Rural postal abbr.
16 Destroy, as documents
19 Dubious gift
22 Famous "No, No, Nanette" number
24 Seriously suggest
25 Eyes, in a certain Christmas song
26 Gloomy
27 Rice whose characters have blood lust?

DOWN

1 Doesn't just sit around and do nothing
2 "The Music Man" setting
3 First-person shooter that gives me a little motion sickness
4 Best Will Ferrell movie, don't @ me
5 Certain Central Park worker
6 "I've got a bad feeling about this ..."
7 Musical based on Fellini's "8½"
8 "Is your wife a ___?" (line from a classic Monty Python skit)
12 Get the better of
15 ___ to (check, as a dictionary)
16 Muffin top?
17 Person with lots of life savings?
18 Prego competitor
19 School across the Thames from Windsor
20 "Black ___" (Natalie Portman film)
21 Marie Curie, by birth
23 Company that was a demonstrator at the 1939 World's Fair

by Patrick Blindauer

ACROSS

1 Lox bagel bits
7 With 1-Down, first Black woman in congress
8 Unnecessary Zooms, e.g.
11 Sugar suffix
12 Say, "I choose me," perhaps
13 Top degs.
15 Hindu goddess in the Ramayana
16 As of now
18 OK clock setting
19 Get taken down a notch
21 Man who goes to Washington in a 1939 film
22 It's all in the past

DOWN

1 With 7-Across, she who said, "If they don't give you a seat at the table, bring a folding chair"
2 Set one's sights on
3 War starter?
4 "All ___ being equal ..."
5 Steed checks
6 Cartel
7 Things on a bus route
9 Bit of camp
10 New York, but not Seattle
14 Fresh
17 San ___, Italy
20 Tree that comes in red, white, and silver

by Juliana Tringali Golden

ACROSS

1 Pre-Euro Florentine coin
5 Cartoon fight sound effect
8 Pinching crustacean or a grump
9 Position for a building
10 Hip-hop artist who doubles as a 7× NBA All-Star
12 Original note sounded by the Liberty Bell before it cracked
13 Concert perk, perhaps
16 "No introduction needed" phrase
17 Star of the 2005 film "Pride & Prejudice"
22 Column in a baseball box score
23 A few, but not many
24 Highly successful French soccer club, familiarly
25 Word after Disney or Discovery in subscription streaming service offerings

DOWN

1 Flat-panel TV type
2 Glass in a recording studio
3 Strike solidly
4 "The Simpsons" grandfather
5 Debtors' mail
6 Mountain range of North Africa
7 What an Impossible Burger lacks
9 Chesterfield, for example
11 ___ perception
13 Serena's older sister
14 Chatting online, for short
15 Tent fasteners
16 Cincinnati radio station of TV
18 Baking powder amount: Abbr.
19 "That's funny," in a text
20 Bird seen in Liberty Mutual ads
21 Progressive rock band with hits in the '70s and '80s

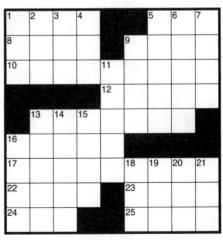

by Adesina O. Koiki

ACROSS

1 Acclaimed 1952 John Ford film, with "The"
9 Screened, as a film
11 On and on and on and on and on and on
12 Feature of a j but not a J
13 Boundaries between astrological signs
14 Kraken's league
15 ___ White ("Dreamgirls" role)
18 Pod veggie
21 Piñata-whacking accessory
23 Hybrid string instrument
24 1973 Billy Joel hit

DOWN

1 View from a dorm
2 Mistake-fixing command
3 "It just ___ done"
4 Gp. administered by Michael S. Regan
5 Alluded to
6 Metropolis in northern Iraq
7 They're often blonde
8 ___ tide
10 You might slide into them online
14 Sneaky warrior
15 Decline
16 Cat's passageway through a door
17 Over, in French
18 Amanda Gorman creation
19 Scat singer Fitzgerald
20 Yemeni city whose harbor is in a volcanic crater
22 "Right Round" rapper ___ Rida

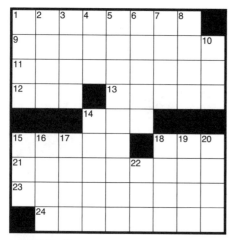

by Will Nediger

ACROSS

1 Like Brie and Camembert cheese
5 Pang of pain
9 Grammy-winning 2019 album by Tyler, the Creator
10 Donkey's cry
11 Complex that employs residential supervisors
13 "Earth to ___" (Disney+ series that premiered in 2020 and was unceremoniously removed in 2023)
14 Some weather forecast figures
15 Swiss ___ (leafy vegetable)
17 Twelve-inch measurement
18 Blue

21 Social networking app that features "rooms" with audio chats
23 Sage, dill, or thyme, e.g.
24 Who a TA assists
25 Like granola and Cheerios
26 Up in the air

DOWN

1 The S of ASL
2 Fairy tale beast
3 Section in many an airport terminal
4 ___ TV ("Impractical Jokers" channel)
5 Passionately hate

6 Move with the music?
7 Razzie Award contenders, say
8 Potato growth
12 Poet who wrote "I am a mountain now, among mountainy women"
16 Crossword puzzling, perhaps
17 Wingless bloodsucker
19 Starting on
20 Refuse to obey
21 Sulu portrayer John
22 Big brand of nail polish

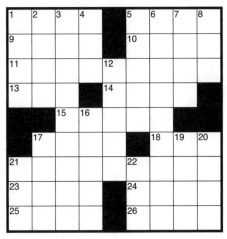

by Andrew J. Ries

ACROSS

1 Came home, in a way
5 Steven Spielberg title character of 1975
9 "Did it!"
10 Got off one's high horse, perhaps
11 With 24-Across, slogan of the Three Musketeers
13 Louisiana marshland
14 Spain's Olympics code
15 Pt. of a flight plan
17 "A Hymn to ___" ("My Fair Lady" song)
20 Salsa, for one
24 See 11-Across
26 Sudden desire
27 Gem whose name is thought to come from the Sanskrit for "precious stone"
28 Take in some Tolkien, for example
29 Poland Spring alternative

DOWN

1 Stick with a fork
2 "___ Land"
3 How doodles are usually drawn
4 Willem of "The Fault in Our Stars"
5 Peter Pan is sealed inside one
6 Cold cream additive
7 Has the lowest score, in golf
8 Part of a flight?
12 Perform better than
16 Burr who is portrayed in "Hamilton"
17 Rush ___ (traffic jam puzzle)
18 Concerning, on a memo
19 Prefix with church or millions
21 ___ Valley
22 Dreidel material, in a song
23 Fitzgerald who won 13 Grammys (plus a Lifetime Achievement Award)
25 Took to Church's, for instance

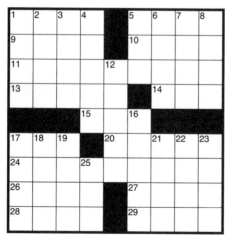

by Patrick Blindauer

ACROSS

1 Skin soother
5 Seek consent
8 Birthing assistant
10 Warm embrace
11 With 3-Down, groundbreaking book about health and sexuality
13 Only
14 Over again
16 Drop-down list
20 Sun god worshipped in "Raised by Wolves"
21 With 19-Down, message of a 1960s feminist movement
22 Over-parent, maybe
24 Polish brand with shades like "15 Minutes of Flame"
25 They might say "Hello" from the other side
26 Bit of ink
27 Destination for lovebirds?
28 Spanish letter after "ka"

DOWN

1 Fuss
2 Civil rights activist Fannie ___ Hamer
3 See 11-Across
4 Macaroni shape
5 Fish in a tuna roll
6 WNBA star Bird who's engaged to Megan Rapinoe
7 Metric wts.
9 Early email domain
12 Free download, often
14 Poetically pale
15 "... said ___ ever"
17 Make it melodrama
18 Tibet neighbor
19 See 21-Across
21 Wickedly funny
23 CPR expert

by Juliana Tringali Golden

ACROSS

1 "___ out" (long-held football axiom regarding field goal kicking)
6 Hog haven
9 Small bell instrument with origins in Yoruba music
10 Adverb that sounds like a number
11 Divided island in the Malay Archipelago
12 Hartsfield-Jackson airport code
13 Chemical suffix
14 Canoe that travels both directions?
16 Become hot, in a way
18 Last hurdle of a semester
19 Alternative to satellite
21 Complaint, informally
24 ___ gras
25 Hogwarts librarian Pince
26 "Rosanna" rock group
27 Model seen in science classrooms

DOWN

1 How one may "fashionably" arrive to a party
2 You cannot avoid it
3 "That's absurd!"
4 A conscious thinking subject, in metaphysics
5 "The West Wing" creator Aaron
6 "Keep your eyes peeled!"
7 Damage beyond repair
8 "Sunny" part of a breakfast
15 Peninsula with seven countries
17 YouTube rival
19 Toward the stern of a ship
20 ___ goo gai pan
22 Angsty rock or rap genre
23 Relatives or close friends, casually

by Adesina O. Koiki

ACROSS

1 "The Handmaid's Tale" protagonist
7 Photocopies
9 Less pleasant to be around
11 "___ you for real?"
12 Economist Emily who wrote "Cribsheet"
14 Sauce that might be "alla bolognese"
16 Masking material
17 "Still da Baddest" rapper
19 Hockey parent's ride
20 Seashell or ivory
22 Not as fresh?
23 Gibson of the "Fast & Furious" films

DOWN

1 Bovine-powered vehicle
2 Geraldine who ran for vice president in 1984
3 Redundant offering in many ads
4 Landmark reproductive rights decision (while it lasted)
5 Really big show
6 Rationalistic believer in God
8 Ignore for now
10 Considers (to be)
13 Worship
15 Not likely to make the cut
18 Haywire
21 "I don't know ___" (phrase in a Mariah Carey meme)

by Will Nediger

ACROSS

1 Drag-increasing airplane wing parts
6 Gives a push to
8 Like a perfect plan
10 Gymnast Raisman with six Olympic medals
11 The Spartans of the Big 10: Abbr.
12 Red-tinged type of lunar eclipse
16 Aid for doing some digging
17 Dreariness felt by some video conferencing users, say
23 Neighbor of Minnesota
24 With 15-Down, "fishy" diner orders
25 At that time
26 Dance move

DOWN

1 Ice cream alternative, informally
2 "Hahaha"
3 TikTok, for one
4 Each
5 Decreased-speed replay, for short
6 Subject of FiveThirtyEight analysis
7 Just average
8 Amazing, say
9 Partner of games
13 "Holy moly!"
14 Focus for some sitters
15 See 24-Across
17 Skin blemish
18 Bit of fireworks show commentary
19 "What do I ___ you?"
20 Magazine owned by Equal Pride
21 Number frequently worn by hockey goalies
22 Park reference

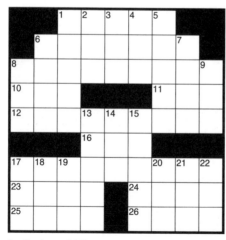

by Andrew J. Ries

ACROSS

1. ___ mode (energy-saving car setting)
4. Leader leader?
9. Cell service icon
10. Festival of Colors celebrant
11. With 24- and 15-Across, quote from "Hamlet"
13. It may help you reach new heights
14. Had breasts, say
15. See 11-Across
17. Psychic power, for short
20. "Save the ___ for your momma"
24. See 11-Across
26. Cornrow covering, perhaps
27. Construction zone smell
28. Drywall supports
29. Yoko who suggested "Go to the middle of the Central Park Pond and drop your jewelry"

DOWN

1. Recedes, as the tide
2. Don't put it in front of the horse, they say
3. Classic Blizzard flavor, though I'm a big fan of Snickers at the moment
4. Stadium fare topped with beef and beans
5. Smash success
6. Grammy-winning singer of "A Day Without Rain"
7. Work at a copy desk
8. Sneaky trick
12. Part of a wedding ceremony
16. ___TV ("Tacoma FD" network)
17. LAX guesstimates
18. Last word in the title of Kubrick's last film
19. Lima is its capital
21. Saxophone that's smaller than a tenor
22. Sound of pleasure or pain
23. ___-Cuban (music genre)
25. Having a bawl?

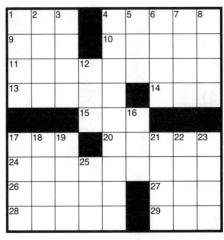

by Patrick Blindauer

ACROSS

1 Married
4 Sheep-speak
7 Before now
8 "Don't mind ___ do"
9 Act of aggression?
13 Nickname for Sean Bean's "Game of Thrones" character
14 Cardinals, on scoreboards
15 Retrogress
17 Org. that makes people remove their shoes
18 "The Problem With ___" (documentary about a South Asian "Simpsons" character)
19 Howard of "Arrested Development"
20 Everlasting
24 Very low-key
25 Bit on a bun

DOWN

1 2020 summer single by Cardi B and Megan Thee Stallion
2 Latin for I
3 Plunges
4 Finch fodder
5 Fore opposite on a boat
6 Classic RV brand
10 Fair hiring abbr.
11 "Put your wallet away"
12 Start to grow?
15 Chasm
16 Reveal, poetically
21 One of the Three Stooges
22 Promos and pop-ups
23 Gun lobbying gp. that filed for bankruptcy in January 2021

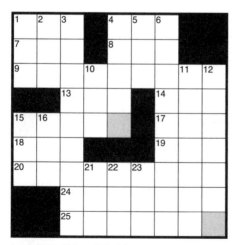

by Juliana Tringali Golden

ACROSS

1 CBS drama revolving around forensics
4 Defeated cry
9 Succor
10 Shade of blue
11 Win a game immediately after losing one's serve, in tennis
13 Famed fratricide fatality
14 Smartphone notifications
18 NCAA D1 hockey conference where Ivy League schools make up half its members: Abbr.
21 What a baserunner is deemed when struck by a batted ball in fair territory
22 Piece of equipment that improves posture
25 Like the name Rose, for a florist
26 Opera character who kills a police chief
27 Flunky's usual response
28 Up to (a certain time)

DOWN

1 Alternative to a zin
2 ___ Mix-a-Lot (Seattle-based rapper with a 1992 megahit)
3 Patent's basis
4 "Family Matters" nerd (and not his narcissistic alter ego)
5 Earl, for example
6 Modern self-preservation initialism
7 Insect-secreted substance used to make varnish and sealing wax
8 Wapiti
12 How the surprised are taken
15 Criticize severely
16 Actor Stanley
17 Eye-opening bargain
18 It was known as AuctionWeb from 1995 to 1997
19 Batgirl garb
20 New Testament book, informally
23 Air-conditioning measure: Abbr.
24 Director Howard

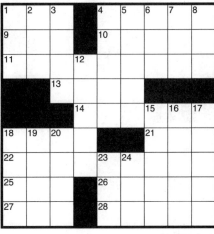

by Adesina O. Koiki

ACROSS

1 "Excuse me ..."
5 They're sung to the tune of "Twinkle, Twinkle, Little Star"
9 Condition in many a soap opera
10 Move in some board games
11 Annoying sound from a faucet
12 Member of a TikTok subculture
13 "Minnie the Moocher" singer Cab
15 Female Cheviot
16 Virginia Woolf protagonist Clarissa
21 Cubes in some board games
22 Anti-police activist Mariame
23 Pavlova or Paquin
24 From the top
25 What feuding people have
26 TALK LIKE THIS

DOWN

1 "Stiff Upper Lip" band
2 1982 Israeli Eurovision entry named for a dance
3 Pessimistic author Cioran
4 Symbol on the Canadian flag
5 Text from an anxious romantic partner
6 Bubble tea
7 Be overly sweet
8 Cunning
14 Bird represented by an Ookpik
16 Have a banquet
17 Common cause of self-esteem issues
18 Go down, as interest
19 Brother of Cain
20 Type of boat that sounds like a pronoun
21 Small amount of paint

by Will Nediger

ACROSS

1 Name that's an anagram of "Lisa"
5 Exam for an aspiring doctor: Abbr.
9 Drummer's rhythm
10 County in Ohio, Pennsylvania, and New York
11 Milkshake cousin
12 Male turkeys
13 Feeling of dizziness
15 Tool for cleaning a litter box
16 Alcoholic drink served in a to-go cup, in modern parlance
19 Brainstorm production
20 House group, for short
22 Interpret
23 Logician's transition
24 Burnt ___ (barbecue joint dish)
25 "Now!"

DOWN

1 Tech company nicknamed "Big Blue"
2 Emmy winner Remini
3 Tip for a marketer
4 Commercials that smear a political rival
5 Region that includes a city and its suburbs
6 Workers who use rakes
7 Gets the crosshairs lined up
8 Composer/news anchor John
14 Period, essentially
16 Electrician's spool
17 City in Yemen on its namesake gulf
18 Lydia Ko was its 2022 Player of the Year: Abbr.
21 Soak (up)

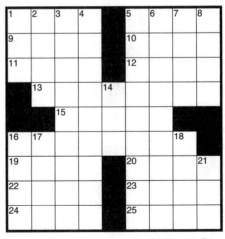

by Andrew J. Ries

ACROSS

1 The English channel?
4 Sunnis and Sufis, e.g.
9 Atop, poetically
10 Love in Lanai
11 Punk band that recorded "Scream" in 1984
13 ___, Bravo, Charlie
14 Extra NBA periods
15 Since Jan. 1
16 Insta messages
17 Rockefeller center?
18 Bug tail?
20 K-pop band that recorded "Ice Cream" in 2020
23 Idaho capital
24 Paris pal
25 Word before can or tan
26 Michelle Obama ___ Robinson

DOWN

1 Tapioca pearl
2 Swimming pool fail
3 Place to purchase handmade goods
4 Aptly named handbag brand, with "the"
5 One of Santa's little helpers
6 Like some coffee beans
7 "My bad"
8 Droops
12 Scoundrel
16 Fist bump
17 Flows back
19 Depression-era migrant
21 Farm box letters
22 Crucial

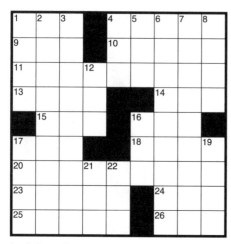

by Juliana Tringali Golden

ACROSS

1 "This royally, indubitably blows!," in textspeak
4 Make noises like a dove
7 Not ordained
8 Attila or one of his followers
9 Inscribe
11 ___ mortals (insignificant beings)
12 ___ pie (cream-filled chocolate cake)
14 "Power" channel
15 What might happen at an Irish pub if St. Patrick's Day festivities get too rowdy
17 Liking very much
20 It was knocked off one's shoulder as an agreement to engage in a fight, per 19th-century U.S. custom
22 Actress Dee of "Do the Right Thing"
23 Trevi Fountain monies, once
24 1998 DreamWorks film with buggy animation

25 Vampire Weekend singer Koenig

DOWN

1 Traveled like a monarch?
2 "Do the ___!"
3 Web portal launched in 1994
4 Popular topping seen on heroes (err, I mean hoagies) regularly served up at Pat's or Geno's
5 "___ Flag Means Death"
6 Any nonzero number raised to the power of zero
10 1999 Missy Elliott chart-topper
11 Act of God
13 Equal level
16 Train from Penn Station to the Hamptons: Abbr.
17 Rollover acronym
18 Jessica Lange, in "American Horror Story: Asylum"
19 Hashtag paired with uploaded pictures featuring people wearing acid-washed jeans, perhaps
21 Chicken à la king ingredient

by Adesina O. Koiki

ACROSS

1 Dog that's easy to confuse with a mop

5 Sleep apnea treatment, briefly

9 "Like that's ever gonna happen"

10 Bum, in Britain

11 Soft mineral

12 "Jeopardy!" champion Jackson

13 German art songs

15 Playwright Parks who wrote "Topdog/Underdog"

18 "No more!"

19 Rivers, in Spanish

20 State that looks like a rectangle that's partly covered by Wyoming

24 "This meme is so relatable"

25 Japanese soup seasoning

26 Admit everything, with "up"

27 Dog originating from China, casually

DOWN

1 Square of butter

2 Today preceder

3 ___ Kim

4 Parts of conditional sentences

5 Storage spot in the desert

6 Museum with lots of Goyas

7 Flower whose name means "star"

8 ___ dish

14 Gerund suffix

15 Letter attachment

16 Stick together

17 Many modern meetings

21 It might be skinny

22 Pose during a Q&A

23 Tool for weeding

by Will Nediger

ACROSS

1 Have a sample of
4 Add fuel to, as a fire
9 ___ Speedwagon
10 Be like a helicopter parent
11 Ward under close watch: Abbr.
12 "Gladiator" setting
13 West Virginia senator Joe
15 Take a couple jabs, perhaps
16 Corrin who won a Golden Globe for "The Crown" in 2021
19 Big house
21 Fabric named for a Scandinavian country
23 Yank
24 Paperless option on Tax Day
25 Oklahoma City Thunder point guard ___ Mann
26 Lugged
27 Platform for many sketches, for short

DOWN

1 Fixes for bad haircuts
2 Sum up
3 "The possibilities are endless!"
4 Title from the Persian for "king"
5 Boris Johnson and Theresa May, for two
6 Pan handling items?
7 Half of a repetitively named numbers game
8 The E of BCE
14 Baby bed
17 Feel sorrow
18 Investor in a start-up, perhaps
20 Luxury opposite
21 Division of a tennis match
22 Sighting that may turn out to be a weather balloon

by Andrew J. Ries

ACROSS

1 Beach physique
4 Ctrl-___-del
7 Sea-turned-desert in Kazakhstan
9 Knocks dead
11 San ___ (Italian resort)
12 Came down to earth
13 "Have a great trip!"
15 One billion years
16 Shore things
22 Carefully cut
23 Fire powder?
24 China setting
25 It's quite the tale
26 Take a taste
27 Free-all link

DOWN

1 "___ and 21-Down Go to Vista Del Mar"
2 Iconic sandwich cookie
3 Jinx, biblically
4 Distant state?
5 Lady who "walks like a woman and talks like a man" in a Kinks song
6 Bit of a branch
8 Sofa for two
10 Business card abbreviation
14 "That's so cool!"
16 Beauty spot?
17 Peace of mind
18 Soprano's solo
19 Laze about
20 Nike's Swoosh, e.g.
21 "1-Down and ___ Go to Vista Del Mar"

by Juliana Tringali Golden

ACROSS

1 Apple core?
4 Swag, briefly
9 Already on fire
10 Advil alternative
11 Oscar-winning actor Mahershala
12 ___ Franklin, American swimmer who won four gold medals at the 2012 Summer Olympics at age 17
13 Stand-up routine, typically
15 Mix (in), as when following a recipe
16 Tiny landmass
19 Feature of many a pro wrestling match ... or the stars of a popular Geico commercial ("Scoop! There it is!")
21 Cost of something
23 The Diamondbacks, on baseball scoreboards
24 Financial return
25 Police dept. member
26 Grandma ___ (artist who started her painting career as a septuagenarian)
27 Oui, on the other side of La Manche

DOWN

1 Form of social distinction
2 Initial TV episode
3 Public services
4 One of a baby's first words
5 Evoke, as a response
6 Has a clear conscience, say
7 Drugstore chain with a heart logo
8 Attention-getting interjection
14 Ancient source of predictions
17 "___ and in charge"
18 Gives off
20 High school diploma equivalents
21 Dr. Hank ___ (alter ego of Ant-Man)
22 Brazilian resort city, for short

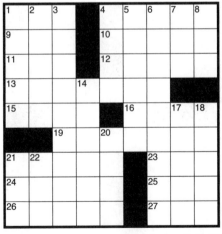

by Adesina O. Koiki

ACROSS

1 Goes (for)
5 One of two for the Moderna vaccine
9 Bird on a Canadian dollar
10 Dips of the head
11 Bird that lived on Mauritius
12 "Ah, gotcha"
13 Takes where the camera gradually moves in
15 Song with a great beat
16 Was no longer on full alert
22 Approximately
23 Second emperor in the Year of the Four Emperors
24 Needing directions
25 1960s muscle cars
26 Type of cyberattack, for short
27 "Golly!"

DOWN

1 Boomers, to millennials
2 Source of trouble, in a song from "The Music Man"
3 Heading on a list
4 Post-fall (in two different senses) clothing items
5 Rapper who briefly renamed himself after a lion
6 Treat with a spiral pattern
7 Leslie ___ Jr. ("One Night in Miami ..." co-star)
8 Clucks of disapproval
14 Supervillain from Krypton
16 Shout accompanied by a gavel strike
17 Stepped
18 ___ buco
19 Bottom center?
20 "___ there?"
21 Snack

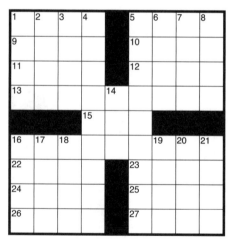

by Will Nediger

ACROSS

1 Pronoun that's the title of songs by Selena Gomez and Harry Styles, among others
4 With 21-Across, Israeli metropolis
7 Part creator
9 Naked
10 Opera singer's performance
11 x, y, or z, in math
12 2013 horror film whose title evokes nighttime
14 Land tract seen inside the word "clearing"
15 Knit headwear that takes its name from a Crimean locale
21 See 4-Across
22 Wrapped up
23 "___ Lisa"
24 What a tomato grows on
25 Shock's partner
26 Works out 2 + 2 = 4, perhaps

DOWN

1 Huge amount
2 "Hava Nagila" dance
3 Kuwaiti head of state
4 Shout from one wanting a pick-me-up
5 Lake at the south end of the Detroit River
6 Word often misused instead of "fewer"
8 Pastry with nuts and honey
9 Actress Maria nominated for an Oscar in 2021 for "Borat Subsequent Moviefilm"
13 One of sixty in a minute, for short
15 "The Tide" of college sports, to fans
16 Profess
17 Formation of waiters
18 Gung-ho
19 Sell
20 God of war in Greek mythology

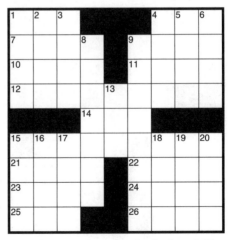

by Andrew J. Ries

117

ACROSS

1 Base × height, for a parallelogram
5 Green standard?
8 Dahl who wrote "The BFG"
10 "___ you for real?"
11 Car company named for a Serbian inventor
12 Tiny taste
13 Happy expression
14 Dead end (and beginning)
15 When the stars come out
18 In the before times
19 Tease a little
20 "Baby Cobra" comic Wong
21 All thumbs
24 Opposite of 22-Down
25 Fall fruits
26 Collectible game piece of the '90s
27 The shape of water?

DOWN

1 "___ is eternal, but life is short": Evelyn De Morgan
2 Maki topper
3 Chill
4 One worshipped by Rumi
5 Adorable bamboo chomper
6 Flounder's friend
7 Push away
9 Brief getaway
15 Org. cofounded by Ida B. Wells
16 Inuit dwelling
17 Made pay
22 Opposite of 24-Across
23 Baker's shortening?

by Juliana Tringali Golden

ACROSS

1 Subject of a 1982 bestseller on sexuality
6 Ranking high on the Scoville scale
9 The only monosyllabic U.S. state
10 Text-scanning technology: Abbr.
11 It's a boring thing
12 Expression of surprise
13 "___ bin ein Berliner": JFK
14 Kingdom of horsemen in "The Lord of the Rings"
16 Bruce of martial arts and cinematic fame
17 Without stopping
18 Main artery of the human body
20 Anti-DUI group
22 Catalog cosmetics brand
25 Changed by time
26 The lone soccer player to win three FIFA World Cup trophies
27 Cones' optical partners
28 19-Down and ___

DOWN

1 Alternative to Microsoft Outlook
2 Chermoula or piri piri
3 Stupidly stubborn
4 "Back at ___" (1999 R&B hit by Brian McKnight)
5 Awful fear
6 State of complete happiness
7 Billy who scored three #1 songs in the U.S. in the 1980s
8 Tendency
15 Recorded, in a way
19 ___ and 28-Across
20 Tarnish
21 Before the present
23 Antiquated
24 Sega Genesis competitor: Abbr.

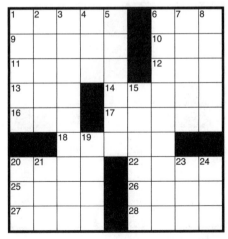

by Adesina O. Koiki

ACROSS

1 "Ladies and gentlemen, the weekend!"
5 Functions
9 Sport with yokozuna
10 ___ and parcel
11 Ingredient in some jellies
12 "E lucevan le stelle," e.g.
13 Rifling (through)
15 Soprano Sumac
16 Gender identity for some Native Americans
22 Tribe surrounded by the Navajo Nation
23 Zippo
24 Like leap years
25 Ikea manual component
26 Department store department
27 Twinings products

DOWN

1 Title for Boris Godunov
2 "Beyond the Lights" star Mbatha-Raw
3 Salat leader
4 As a punishment, facetiously
5 Confronting
6 Draped garment
7 Burnett or Brockovich
8 Without a date
14 Box at a concert
16 They/___
17 Made baskets
18 Accepting customers
19 Quote from a freelancer
20 Reason to cry "Eureka!"
21 Advances, as for a job

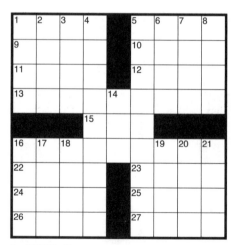

by Will Nediger

ACROSS

1 Authorizes
4 Touchdown spot in Boston
9 Top seed
10 "Schitt's Creek" Emmy winner
11 FTW locale
13 Kristen of "Barb and Star Go to Vista Del Mar"
14 Division that contained the WFT (now the Commanders)
18 Drops from above
19 "WTF" host
24 Hawaiian for "compassion"
25 "When will you be here?" in texts
26 Cross-promotional marketing ploy
27 Nebraska senator Fischer

DOWN

1 "That hurt!"
2 Widely recognized
3 Flourish of a printed letter
4 European language with a "High" counterpart
5 "Lookie what we have here!"
6 Fish with a long nose
7 Class in a studio
8 "I'll pass"
12 Spasm
15 TV remote battery, perhaps
16 Fathered
17 Government-issued bond, for short
19 Item by a door
20 Muhammad or Mahershala
21 Landmark 1973 case, familiarly
22 X in the Greek alphabet
23 Snag

by Andrew J. Ries

ACROSS

1 Word before run or jump
4 Eight, en español
8 Enormous stretches of time
10 Nation formerly known as Persia
11 Kitty in the garden?
13 Issa of "Insecure"
14 Payment to the IRS
15 Kitty in the water?
17 Pacific tuna
18 Big letters in root beer
19 Kitty in the weeds?
23 Geometric measure
24 TV sports award
25 Discovery in a murder mystery
26 Open ___ night

DOWN

1 Game, ___, match
2 Colorful Japanese fish
3 Deeply rooted
4 First ingredient in a stir fry
5 Foundation of a film review
6 Prepared according to Muslim law
7 Black stone
9 Flight selection
12 Knot again
15 Spanish singer and frequent guest on "RuPaul's Drag Race"
16 Up to the task
17 "Just ___" ("Not too much")
20 Calendar square
21 Big letters in nail polish
22 MoMA metropolis

by Juliana Tringali Golden

ACROSS

1 Unfriendly
4 Resort for rejuvenation
7 ___ change
8 "Split" vegetables
9 Bounding sidewalk activity during the summer, perhaps
12 Penn of the Harold & Kumar films
13 Soft woven fabric with ribs
16 Editing technique where one continuous shot is broken into two parts by removing frames in between
17 Contacted via one's "Buddy List" on AOL, for short
18 Not that
21 ___ cava (heart feeder)
22 Remove, as pressure
23 Vortex in a stream
24 "Game of Thrones" surname

DOWN

1 Suffix meaning "to some extent"
2 Oprah, to OWN
3 Shrill dog sound
4 Where a television show is shot
5 ___-12 (league with a Final Four)
6 ___ Barty, who retired in 2022 while she was the #1-ranked women's tennis player in the world
8 Contaminates
10 American "tradition" where seniors play hooky en masse (Thanks, Ferris Bueller!)
11 AP math class, for short
13 Was irate
14 Modify, as a law
15 Actor Hawke
16 Jazz music style originating in the '30s
19 One-on-one situation, in basketball slang
20 Work with needles and thread

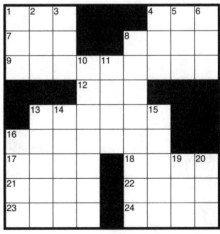

by Adesina O. Koiki

ACROSS

1 "Hateship, Friendship, Courtship, ___, Marriage" (Alice Munro story)
9 Identified with a finger
11 In the direction of the beach
12 Like a limbo bar
13 Feline zodiac sign
14 Reach across
16 Rudely dismissive
17 "It ___ a nice ring to it"
18 Short form that omits "-utation" or "-resentative"
19 Out-of-place occurrences
23 He studied under Balenciaga
24 TV show set on the Pacific Princess, with "The"

DOWN

1 Full-blown albums
2 "Intriguing!"
3 Chance for William Primrose to shine
4 Company that went bankrupt in 2001
5 Instant Pot creation
6 Stick closely (to)
7 First woman to direct a film noir (1953's "The Hitch-Hiker")
8 Cutter in the kitchen
10 Toronto, slangily
14 Fish with valuable roe
15 Group of speakers
16 One who once had a verified blue check on Twitter, maybe
18 Like two-headed snakes
20 Kyrie Irving or Luka Dončić, casually
21 When you think you'll get there, briefly
22 Plopped down

by Will Nediger

ACROSS

1 Two queens, perhaps
5 It's used by a maple syrup maker
8 Muppet who speaks in the third person
9 Bonefishes' cousins
10 "But no ..."
11 Staple foods in West Africa
12 Unexciting quality
14 One who doesn't share
15 Spinning
20 Funny saying
21 "I know it only too well"
22 Addresses displayed in many ads
23 Tree that produces a butter nut
24 Frequently
25 Categorize ... and, when read differently, the letters that can go in the shaded squares

DOWN

1 Green production on some farms
2 Penne ___ vodka (Italian dish)
3 Prayer leader
4 Fleshy parts of a certain flower
5 Word that can follow "high"
6 Charitable givings
7 Additions at the ends of letters: Abbr.
9 Monocle
13 Companion of "neither"
15 Part of a rhyming meat-and-seafood dinner order
16 Go limp
17 "I think ...", to a texter
18 ___-do-well (no-goodnik)
19 Pesky bug
20 Status ___

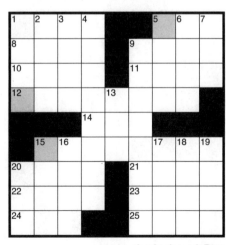

by Andrew J. Ries

ACROSS

1 Prof's degree
4 Channel that frequently features commentary from Ben Mankiewicz
7 Home ground
9 Stark sister on "Game of Thrones"
11 Intellectuality
13 Charitable person
14 Ave. crossers
15 Genre for Selena Montgomery (a.k.a. Stacey Abrams)
17 Take a turn?
18 Something unpleasant that always turns up, so the saying goes
22 One with two matches?
23 Existed

DOWN

1 Condition that may follow an ordeal: Abbr.
2 Genre for Rachel Bloom
3 Liquid–Plumr rival
4 Get some sun
5 Banana shape
6 Genre for Tana French
8 Word on a gift tag
10 Wise-___
12 Genre for Monisha Rajesh
16 State bird of Hawaii
18 "Oh, and another thing": Abbr.
19 Exist
20 N, E, S, or W
21 Masks, gloves, etc.: Abbr.

by Juliana Tringali Golden

ACROSS

1 App with filters, for short
6 Tacit assent
9 "Not in your life!"
10 Yellowfin tuna in Hawaii
11 Lofty aspiration
12 A-lister
13 Over there, in verse
14 You can "walk the dog" with one
16 "Stepping away for a moment," briefly
17 Third word in many limericks
20 One of two in an oboe's mouthpiece
22 Word repeated before "Read all about it"
24 Pro Football Hall of Fame wide receiver Monk
26 Braided hair
27 Neither companion
28 Durations in office
29 Person who works with bugs?

DOWN

1 Home to "the Greatest Spectacle in Racing," informally
2 Fictional crime-solver Wolfe
3 "Frozen" reindeer
4 Green or black beverage
5 Some well-traveled children, perhaps
6 Common soup legumes
7 It's high in the middle and round at both ends, in an old joke
8 Downturn
15 Calif. neighbor
17 Bawled
18 Wheel-connecting rod
19 It's added to a country's official soccer badge after winning a World Cup
21 Pull out of, as a class you don't want affecting your GPA
23 Outer edge
25 Attempt

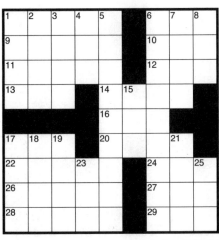

by Adesina O. Koiki

ACROSS

1 Holes
5 Piece of stock foot-age?
9 Speed skater with the middle name Anton
11 Combo of salad greens
12 Many physics homework assignments, casually
13 Pigpen
14 "___ Found Now" (2013 My Bloody Valentine song)
16 Reddit Q&A
19 "The Memory Police" author Yoko
23 Combo of freezing rain, ice pellets, and snow
25 Using a certain form of birth control
26 Unlikely to volunteer
27 Head of Haiti?

DOWN

1 "Holy moly!"
2 Phone downloads
3 Sweat producer
4 Incisions made with letter openers
5 Refuse to share
6 Resistance measurements
7 "I'll get to work right now!"
8 ___ Brown (Pam Grier role)
10 Off the boat
15 Umm Kulthum's home country
16 Nowhere to be found
17 Sports journalist Kimes
18 Movie that improbably came out the same year as "A Bug's Life"
20 French friend
21 Droop
22 Part connected to a chassis
24 Your, old-style

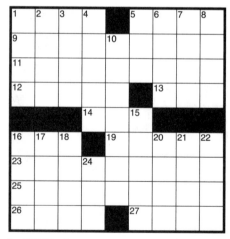

by Will Nediger

ACROSS

1 Chairman of the Climate Reality Project
7 Boating competition
9 Mineral formation with a rounded shape
11 Ice-melting compound
13 Sequence in computer programming
16 Teacher's lobby: Abbr.
17 As well
18 Winks and hand signals, for example
22 Cartoonist who created Popeye
23 R&B element

DOWN

1 Contemptible person
2 Field of grass
3 Wonder Woman portrayer Gadot
4 Sister brand of Miracle-Gro
5 Weather app feature
6 Cause of some produce recalls
8 Transistor part that sends out particles
10 Group spirit
12 Branch of rap or rock
13 Fire-breathing emotion
14 Hanger-on
15 Full of pomp but little substance, as a speaker
19 Festive occasion in Vietnam
20 "Not again!"
21 Crash into

by Andrew J. Ries

ACROSS

1 FBI division
4 Before 15-Across, sweet temptation
9 Hoppy brew, briefly
10 Martini garnish
11 Animated reboot featuring Huey, Dewey, Louie, Webby, and Della
13 Bit on "A Black Lady Sketch Show"
14 Tree in a horror title
15 Word that completes 3-Down, 4-Across, 21-Down, and 28-Across
17 Engine additive and NASCAR sponsor
20 Speak up
23 Hang out together as buddies
26 Response to "Am not!"
27 Bus. driver?
28 After 15-Across, slow-cooked supper
29 Beer barrel

DOWN

1 "Where ___ Our Love Go?" (1964 hit for the Supremes)
2 Magnum ___ (musical masterwork)
3 Before 15-Across, big prize
4 Gung ho
5 "Hello" in Brazil
6 Egyptian waterway
7 Daredevil Knievel
8 Cowboy's affirmative
12 Laotian currency that's also a nickname
16 Confucian path of enlightenment
17 Train for a match
18 Tasty Tahitian tuber
19 Guilty, not guilty, or no contest
21 After 15-Across, party you might bring a dish to
22 Joint used in a squat
24 Word after smart or dumb
25 Chow chow, e.g.

by Juliana Tringali Golden

ACROSS

1 Enthusiastic greeting
8 "No need to help me out, but thank you anyway!"
10 Notable transformation
11 Tanned skin
12 React to being hit on the head, perhaps
18 ___ Pye (helicopter traffic reporter on "The Simpsons")
19 2008 presidential campaign slogan
23 Visually unappealing
24 Educational acronym
25 Like feet in a yoga class
26 Pothole filler

DOWN

1 Single leaf of grass
2 Toast maker, often
3 Sound heard from a Jacuzzi?
4 Need for translation, in biology
5 ___ Solo
6 Big name in boots
7 "___ whiz!"
8 Suffix meaning "somewhat"
9 Luau wreaths
13 Drain energy out of
14 It is built in a stable relationship
15 Actress Corsaut of "The Andy Griffith Show"
16 University located in Lawrenceville, New Jersey
17 Give the impression
19 Jersey Mike's offering
20 2020, 2022, and 2023 French Open women's singles champion ___ Świątek
21 High-end camera type: Abbr.
22 Calm region at the center of a storm

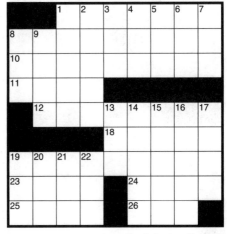

by Adesina O. Koiki

ACROSS

1 Kumbh ___ (major Hindu pilgrimage)
5 One of the Spice Girls
9 "I'm done talking now"
10 Alternative to a recitative
11 Vessel that might be tulip-shaped
13 Beach areas
14 Andersson or Orbison
15 Evasion
21 Nonverbal alternative to "Stop that!"
22 Berry in a sugary bowl
23 Friend, in France
24 One of the Spice Girls
25 Vulcan mind ___

DOWN

1 Does a janitorial job
2 Nickname for Evelyn
3 TV creator Dunham or Waithe
4 One who pronounces on paintings
5 Palindromic language of southern India
6 Time periods
7 Top ten, e.g.
8 Important instrument in funk music
12 ___ two shoes
15 Man expelled from Eden
16 Habit that's best broken
17 Spoken
18 Alaska city with America's largest gold pan
19 Another name for an IUD
20 Squeezed (out)

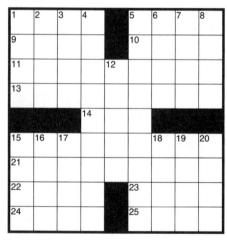

by Will Nediger

ACROSS

1 Natori product
4 Compound in some gummies: Abbr.
7 Sub
9 Crowd chant at the World Cup
10 Sub
12 Grandmother, in British slang
13 Sub ___
15 Early afternoon hour
16 E-newsletter platform ... which 7-, 10-, and 13-Across form in this grid
21 Stoner's exclamation
22 Ball who wrote and directed 2020's "Uncle Frank"
23 Nutritional facts listing
24 Number-picking game
25 Cohort following millennials, for short
26 Make a revision to

DOWN

1 Air conditioner's energy rating measures: Abbr.
2 Country star McEntire
3 Biblical king of Judah
4 Not out in the open
5 Boring, informally
6 Locale for lions
8 Auto part that contacts a brake disc
11 "Deuces," in poker lingo
14 Process of receiving a new patient
16 "You bet"
17 Wheat flour noodles
18 Mercedes-___
19 "Pretty please?"
20 Creation from tying laces
21 Sharp criticism

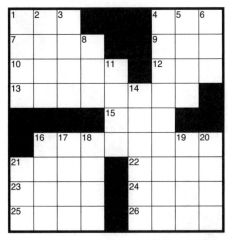

by Andrew J. Ries

ACROSS

1 Biblical language
8 Sunny-day accessory
9 Opening notes?
12 "Home Economics" network
13 Kitchen measurement
14 Treat from a truck
16 NYSE and NASDAQ
17 Palindromic conceptual artist
18 "Rogue ___: A Star Wars Story"
19 Closing note?
23 Study carefully
24 "___! Bring back my girls" (RuPaul upon completing "Drag Race" deliberations)

DOWN

1 Fitting
2 Cry from the stands and/or the stans
3 Phone trios
4 Caribbean ballroom dance
5 "Hold on ___!"
6 Apple platform
7 Got to work, say
10 Pistachio, e.g.
11 Rte. finder
14 Anatomical tip
15 Novelist Patchett
16 Memory muse
18 Kind of exam administered by a dentist or a dean
20 Roman 111
21 Business abbr.
22 Tornado starter?

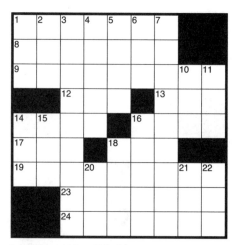

by Juliana Tringali Golden

ACROSS

1 Japanese city on Tokyo Bay
6 Online guffaw
9 "The Inheritance of Loss" author Kiran
10 Santa ___ Mountains
11 Proverbial places of drudgery
13 Exceedingly complicated situation
14 Consume
15 Most heralded performance ... or what the beginning of 13-Across may be?
20 Waikiki Beach location
21 Until 2019, acronym used for the world governing body for the sport of athletics
23 Part of a book jacket
24 Magazine debut of March 3, 1923
25 Cleric's white vestment
26 "Do the ___" (soft drink slogan)

DOWN

1 Bank offerings with fixed terms: Abbr.
2 Use one of the five senses
3 "La ___ Bonita" (1987 Madonna hit)
4 "Next!"
5 Zeroes in on
6 Bowling alley assignment
7 "Hot ___" (YouTube web series involving celebrities eating chicken wings)
8 Endure
12 Know by feeling
15 Site of a crash, perhaps?
16 Like unlikely tales
17 Whaler of literature
18 Popular pest control brand
19 New parent's decision
22 ___ and far between

by Adesina O. Koiki

ACROSS

1 Trade
5 Lettuce variety
9 ___ Caesar (punny salad name)
10 "Do ___ others ..."
11 Chef who hosts "Barefoot Contessa"
13 Sound that betrays someone sneaking downstairs
14 "The Sweet Hereafter" star
17 Page of an old manuscript
18 Book series about people who transform into creatures ... or a hint to 11- and 14-Across
23 Holder in a workshop
24 ___ history (genre for Svetlana Alexievich)
25 Inhabits a role
26 Word in many shampoo commercials

DOWN

1 Take to the slopes
2 Unhealthily pale
3 In the style of
4 Cribbage piece
5 Donkey, in Spanish
6 What a spy gathers
7 Non-starting lineup
8 Knock on the noodle
12 "Gesundheit!" preceder
14 Type of chemical bond
15 Focus of the most attention on the red carpet
16 French city after which denim is named
17 Broad bean
19 Way overcharge
20 Opposite of amateur
21 Ate
22 Sneaky

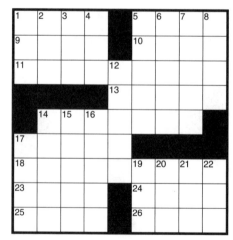

by Will Nediger

ACROSS

1 In addition
5 Vehicle on rails
9 Benefit
10 Surrealist Magritte
11 Congressional positions whose general election races are easy to predict
13 Classification to which all humans belong
14 Famed British reference work: Abbr.
15 Musical with an exclamation point in its title
20 Segment of the Appalachians named for its colorful haze
22 Point after deuce, in tennis
23 Onion relative
24 Do a laundry day task
25 Put cargo on

DOWN

1 Six-pack makeup
2 Garden spread
3 Challenge for movers
4 "Just a second!"
5 Running machine
6 Not fake
7 Start to trust?
8 Landform similar to a butte
12 Attack on one's character
15 Holdings for many CEOs: Abbr.
16 Gucci of fashion
17 "20/20" anchor David
18 Mental concept
19 Sat in a barrel, perhaps
21 Barely make, with "out"

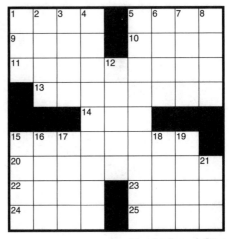

by Andrew J. Ries

ACROSS

1 Soap opera assault
5 James who sang "At Last"
9 Fuzzy little fruit
10 Shakespearean king
11 Mononymous model
12 Not loose
13 With 16-Across, salutation on Star Wars Day
15 Peeped
16 See 13-Across
22 The whole shebang
23 Serpentine swimmers
24 Do some yard work
25 Sat shotgun, perhaps
26 Spilled some plasma
27 They put the "she" in "sheep"

DOWN

1 Flip through
2 Capital of Peru
3 Off on an adventure
4 16 ounces, on this side of the pond
5 Not even close
6 "Roger that"
7 Not loose
8 [External screaming]
14 Word after party or hard
16 Sharp observation?
17 And more, briefly
18 Alert to the intersectionalities of privilege, say
19 "That's hot!"
20 Quaint shoppe word
21 A Swiss Army knife has over 30

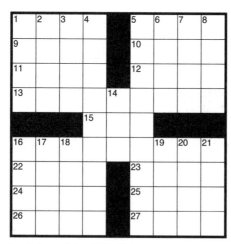

by Juliana Tringali Golden

ACROSS

1 Inflating device
5 ___ Jones
8 George Jetson's four-legged friend
10 Softball slugger's stat
11 With 15-Across, what the day after Star Wars Day represents, to some fans
13 Carolina river named after a Native American tribe
14 "___ further review ..."
15 See 11-Across
19 In a frightened manner
20 Pac-12 school located in Tempe
21 Teen safety organization: Abbr.
22 Hawks or Falcons, on scoreboards
23 Historic opening?

DOWN

1 3, for a short golf hole
2 Take advantage of
3 "I want my ___!" ('80s catchphrase)
4 Person readying oneself for an apocalyptic event
5 Scott who sued for liberty in 1846
6 Double-reed woodwind instrument
7 Soccer player Ali Krieger, to her 2019 USWNT teammate Ashlyn Harris
9 Occurrence that's far from regular
12 "That's so clever!"
14 Moving-day rental
15 Trial run-through
16 What birds' wings do
17 Short response to a long post, in textspeak
18 Jekyll's wild side
19 Flight-regulating organization: Abbr.

by Adesina O. Koiki

ACROSS

1 C section?
4 City north of Des Moines
8 "My compliments to the ___!"
10 Bargain-hunter's destination
11 Unwanted feature of a sock (or necessary feature of a sock)
12 Story
13 Reasons for overtime
15 "Mamma Mia" quartet ... or rhyme scheme of both the top and bottom halves of this grid
16 Arrange for taxi transport
21 Paris's Île de la ___
22 Ice cream holder
23 README file reader
24 Clarinet player's concern
25 Canadian leaders, briefly
26 Wild guess

DOWN

1 German "Oh no!"
2 Difficulty pronouncing R sounds
3 Sworn virgins
4 Danish silent film star Nielsen
5 Polite term of address
6 Reese's role in "Legally Blonde"
7 Catches a glimpse of
9 Not as strong
14 Barn dance participant
17 Parts of plays
18 "Bald" bird
19 "Transit" author Seghers
20 BBC's nickname, with "the"
21 Something raised for a toast

by Will Nediger

ACROSS

1 Minnesota lake that's the source of the Mississippi River
7 Finalized agreement
9 Certain employee benefit
10 Musical role played by Quvenzhané Wallis in a 2014 remake
11 Augmented reality game launched in 2016
16 Kindle download
17 Hair problem ... which can describe the last parts of 9- and 11-Across
21 Reddish members of the salmon family
22 Tribal authorities

DOWN

1 Non-mainstream, say
2 Distance-measuring surveying device
3 Fruit drink
4 Baltic or Adriatic
5 LBJ, at two points in his career
6 Bitter, for one
7 Paul of "There Will Be Blood"
8 Swine farm sound
9 Baby food
12 Complies with
13 ___ of the above
14 Many mythology characters
15 Greenlights
17 Vancouver-to-Seattle direction: Abbr.
18 Mayor or governor, for short
19 TV type: Abbr.
20 Tricky Dick was his veep

by Andrew J. Ries

ACROSS

1 Fancy caramel go-with
8 Beach houses, often
10 Animated
11 Defensive rocket: Abbr.
12 ___-Aztecan languages
13 Chef Rachael
14 Quick stop?
15 "___ Blitz!" (rhyming Yeah Yeah Yeahs album title)
16 Bench press target
17 Where one gets pumped or booted
21 Women who have it all (eventually)
22 Used a certain social app

DOWN

1 Soaks up some rays
2 Land on the other side?
3 Cabinet dept.
4 Yield to gravity
5 Pub order
6 Yoga asana akin to criss-cross applesauce
7 Used a certain social app
8 Predicting a stock market decline
9 Mounted lights
18 Historical period
19 "Gimme a ___!"
20 Sound of disapproval

by Juliana Tringali Golden

142

ACROSS

1 What Roxanne didn't have to put on, in a song by the Police

9 North American–based carrier ... and nickname of future NBA Hall of Famer Vince Carter

10 Paint application devices

11 ___-been

12 Whodunit solver: Abbr.

13 First solo female rapper to release a full album (1988)

16 "On ___ from 1 to 10 ..."

19 Partake in charades, say

23 17th-century Dutch painter

24 "Groove Is in the Heart" group (1990)

DOWN

1 Daytime TV host Kelly

2 Makes a mistake

3 Reagan, on luggage tags

4 Set down

5 Gerund's finish

6 Ostentatious

7 Former name of AXS TV

8 Slight experience

9 Fallout from Eyjafjallajökull

13 Perhaps

14 "You Got Older" playwright Barron

15 8.5″ × 14″ paper size

16 Earth Day mo.

17 Vehicle for a snow day

18 Arrived

20 Folk singer DiFranco

21 Summer hrs. in Denver

22 Summer, in Paris

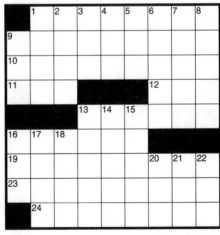

by Adesina O. Koiki

ACROSS

1 Gently pat on the back
5 Experiencing vaccine side effects, perhaps
9 Brief intro to a counterargument
10 Follow one of the Five Pillars of Islam
11 Part of the Bangladeshi diaspora, e.g.
12 Nabisco cracker brand
13 Looking out for number one
15 Young turkey
16 Allergy trigger for some
20 Car
21 Kapolei's island
22 Start to get tired
23 Taking care of the job
24 "About ___" (2009 Asghar Farhadi film)
25 Cuts off, as branches

DOWN

1 Physique, briefly
2 People related to the Chemehuevi
3 Part of a trail leading to a bed, maybe
4 Historically minded study of language
5 Shout after a 4/1 prank
6 Soccer player ___ Ronaldo
7 Possesses, biblically
8 Rush song named for Toronto's airport code
14 Suffix with spoon or fork, but not knife
16 Target of cracking
17 18-Down's bottom
18 Vessel on the waves
19 Nomads' dwellings

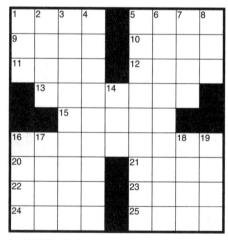

by Will Nediger

144

ACROSS

1 Cases of lentils
5 Refs on a diamond
9 One of the acting Baldwins
10 Grammy winner Anderson .___
11 Salsa alternative with a ketchup-like consistency
13 Game played at a 2019 World Cup competition at New York's Arthur Ashe Stadium
14 Major Muslim holiday
15 Frustration from trying to open packaging
20 The Cyclones of the Big 12
22 Dressed
23 "Westworld" star ___ Rachel Wood
24 Ring items
25 Blend together

DOWN

1 Square of butter
2 Patron saint of Norway
3 Art ___ style
4 Tablets used on game night
5 "Rise 'n shine!"
6 Kahului's island
7 Diplomatic agreement
8 ___-Ball (arcade game)
12 Uses a spoon, in a way
15 String in a candle
16 Part in a movie
17 Not in the office
18 Donated
19 Citation-shortening notation: Abbr.
21 Come to a close

by Andrew J. Ries

ACROSS

1 Spray-paint atomizer
9 Spends some time underground, say
10 Sara Jane Moore, nearly
11 Serpentine letter seen at the start of every clue and at least once in every answer
12 Superlatively wise
17 Sabotages
18 Someone who states something strongly

DOWN

1 Simile segment
2 Some address markers
3 Save for future use
4 Sci-fi weapon
5 Solicitor Tim who moderated "Meet the Press" for over 16 years
6 "Strangers" band The Young'___
7 Schuss or slalom
8 Sister channel of QVC
12 Source of 9-digit IDs
13 Sorority letters
14 Sit-up targets, for short
15 Sault ___ Marie, Michigan
16 Source of the original "Dungeons & Dragons"

This puzzle and the eight following puzzles form a mini meta crossword suite; together, they conceal a two-word phrase that, when correctly interpreted, will lead to an answer phrase that relates to the theme of the final puzzle on page 154.

by Patrick Blindauer

ACROSS

1 Places for diving boards

9 Multiple Emmy winner for "Nick News" Linda

10 Document label

11 Goal for some H.S. dropouts

12 Lengthen

17 Christ the ___ (Rio landmark)

18 Villains, at times

DOWN

1 Rock group ___ Leppard

2 Cornerback Apple

3 Pipe joint with a right angle

4 Capital of Poland?

5 Relative of an osprey

6 Gig for Jazz players?

7 Persephone's mother, who the Romans called Ceres

8 Planting devices

12 Ambulance destinations: Abbr.

13 Longtime "Dancing With the Stars" judge Goodman

14 Poem of praise

15 Jill Biden ___ Jacobs

16 Oktoberfest country: Abbr.

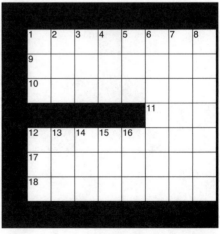

by Patrick Blindauer

ACROSS

1 Docs whose patients may lick them
5 Sports announcer Albert
9 "Tomb Raider" heroine Croft
10 Clarinet's cousin
11 Cell in a fertility clinic
12 1106, in old Rome
13 "___ Out" (Jordan Peele film)
14 Number of Dwarfs + Amigos
15 Save for later, in a way
17 Watching machines?
18 ___ out a living (barely get by)
20 Gourmet
26 2005 Richard Gere movie based on a Myla Goldberg novel
27 Prefix with -mance
28 Sign of success
29 "O Brother, Where ___ Thou?"

DOWN

1 Recurring YouTube journal
2 Having roof extensions
3 Big channel in reality programming
4 Comedian Grittner who tweeted "If my funeral doesn't have a merch table I'm gonna be so freaking pissed"
5 May day honoree
6 "Dancing With the Stars" network
7 Emulates a nomad
8 Streak in blue cheese
16 Goes "Vroom-vroom!"
17 Brand of sport sandals
19 Ukrainian city, in its Russian spelling
20 Org. I threaten to contact when I get bad service but then never do
21 Preposition for a poetic preschool, perhaps?
22 Who Thomas Anderson becomes, in "The Matrix"
23 Butterfield of "Sex Education"
24 Neither's partner
25 Trinitrotoluene, more commonly

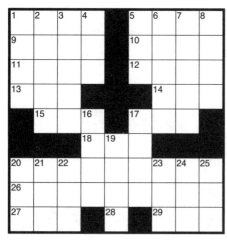

by Patrick Blindauer

ACROSS

1 Certain lifesavers: Abbr.
5 ___ out (chill)
8 Birds a-laying in "The 12 Days of Christmas"
10 Royal Rumble org.
11 1960s show whose star weighed over 500 pounds
13 Start to snow?
14 Finder's ___ (payment made to a middleman)
15 NYPD part: Abbr.
17 Classic comics character Etta, who originally taught good manners
20 Before, to Frost
22 What 28-Across means in English
23 "The Vagina Monologues" playwright
26 Was at the front of the pack
27 They can take the heat, presumably
28 French for 22-Across
29 Direction 90 degrees from norte

DOWN

1 ___ on (incited)
2 Attorney General under Reagan
3 Some classic bikes
4 Plane that traveled approx. 1,350 mph
5 Bugs
6 Baa-maid?
7 Lead-in to X, Y, or Z
9 Best Christmas movie ever made, don't @ me
12 Best thing to shout when you see a mouse, apparently

16 It's between due and quattro
18 Crime in which someone takes something the wrong way?
19 To the point
21 Ltr. addition
23 Architectural addition
24 Formation for migrating 8-Across
25 "___ walks in beauty, like the night / Of cloudless climes and starry skies": Lord Byron

by Patrick Blindauer

ACROSS

1 It's just above where a tag touches
5 Harold's role in "Ghostbusters"
9 Word before fixation or cavity
10 "It's ___ big misunder-standing!"
11 Word from a pen pal?
12 "All done!"
13 Dumfries denial
14 Port of northwest Germany
15 Divided, like a swimming pool
17 Innocent ones
19 ___ so (Shakespearean confirmation)
22 Predecessor of Exxon
23 Pony up, in poker
24 Good name for a mechanic?
25 Cooler brand named for a legendary creature
26 Political cartoonist Thomas
27 Plot in Genesis

DOWN

1 Cinematic showdown time
2 Posh Vegas resort
3 People in discussion groups
4 Rocky Mountain National Park beast
5 Wonderland cake command
6 Made happier
7 Like Seattle's famed Curiosity Shop
8 Bread baked in a tandoor
14 This puzzle has 11, which can be connected by 3 straight lines
16 On the move
17 ___ tetra (aquarium fish)
18 Classic cinematic canine
20 Kitchen fixture?
21 Deutschland denial
23 When repeated, a cry at sea or a primate

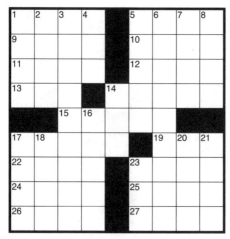

by Patrick Blindauer

ACROSS

1 Like some surgery
8 Start of a popular nighttime song
10 Able to be lit
12 One of the Stooges
13 Actress Ward
14 Manipulate, as a match
15 Letter evoked by this grid's white space
18 Sci. concerned with biomes
19 Detailed
22 Bombers and jets, for example
23 Let go of

DOWN

1 Proper partner
2 Peacock, to NBC
3 Dermatology subject
4 Glide over snow
5 Body image, for short
6 Stork kin
7 Internet-enabled business
9 Boy who befriended E.T.
11 Part of the Anheuser-Busch logo
15 Salutation starter
16 "The Golem" author Wiesel
17 James ___ Jones
18 Periods in the past
20 Letters prior to A.D.
21 "Che ___ è?" ("What time is it?" in Italy)

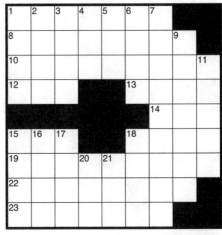

by Patrick Blindauer

ACROSS

1 Tube top awards
6 Certain platters
9 "So do I!"
10 Go on and on and on
11 Folk song featuring a banjo
13 "Time ___ all heels": Groucho Marx in "Go West"
14 Start to freeze?
17 Garment junction
18 Service for an afternoon break
20 Hit single by Steve Perry
24 "The A-Team" muscleman

25 Makeup artists?
26 Take to court
27 Adventure stories

DOWN

1 Genre with a subclass called screamo
2 "I've seen better"
3 The Ozarks, e.g.: Abbr.
4 "Not gonna happen!"
5 Nothing to write home about
6 Jeff of the Traveling Wilburys
7 National Zoo creature

8 Sudden contraction
12 Where Mozart was born
14 Water has three, at the minimum
15 Longest serving prime minister of India
16 "There's no accounting for ___"
19 Coral reef swimmers
21 Dipstick wiper
22 Common savings plan feature
23 One of two in Tuscaloosa

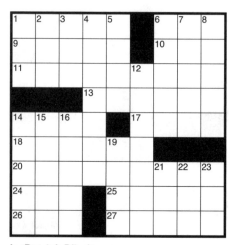

by Patrick Blindauer

ACROSS

1 Persian doctors, say
5 Mode in "The Incredibles"
9 Brand whose recent Chocolate Hazelnut flavor got my interest piqued
10 ___, mean fighting machine
11 With 12-Across, American frontier
12 See 11-Across
13 Come to understand
14 Fathers
15 Takes a turn in a board game
17 Unmovable
19 Groovy music holders?
22 With 23-Across, Monday though Friday
23 See 22-Across
24 Start growing the pot, say
25 Mom's ___ (St. Louis sandwich shop since 1977)
26 Hot follower?
27 Did 40 in a 25 (slow your roll!)

DOWN

1 Rite stuff?
2 "Flagship City"
3 Moves instantly, in sci-fi
4 "___ off!" ("Get lost!")
5 Super Bowl XXXIII MVP John
6 Sound state of slumber
7 Galileo launcher
8 Hill workers
14 ___-Man
16 Gives a thumbs-up, nowadays
17 Did the crawl, say
18 Term that can be musical or muscular
20 Legendary fútbol player
21 Slide sideways on a slippery street
23 Sentence components: Abbr.

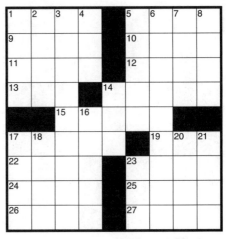

by Patrick Blindauer

ACROSS

1 Tree that sounds like a summer hot spot
4 On-the-go type
9 PhD hopeful's hurdle
10 Draft status?
11 Bud holder
12 What you should probably assume all unsolicited emails are
13 Theoretical physicist Fermi who was not, himself, theoretical
15 "I've never felt so ___"
16 "___-A-Lympics" (Hanna-Barbera spoof of "Battle of the Network Stars")
20 Romantically charm
22 Purplish shade
25 Here, to Matisse
26 Uses as a source
27 People may get it with beans
28 Certain German cars, informally
29 "Who's Afraid of Virginia Woolf?" playwright Edward

DOWN

1 "Saturday Night Fever" group, with "the"
2 Construction site sight
3 Nelly's "Hot in ___"
4 Perfect pear for poaching
5 The ___ (old 7Up nickname)
6 Railroad stop: Abbr.
7 Beta carotene source
8 Microwave oven sounds
14 "You've got some nerve!"
17 Guatemalan girlfriend
18 ___ point
19 Flying saucer
21 Costner's role in "The Untouchables"
22 Blues musician Lee ___
23 "___ High ... Fly-Fight-Win" (motto of the U.S. Air Force)
24 Shoshone relative

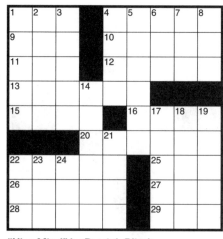

"Hive Mind" by Patrick Blindauer

page 5

S	O	P	H			R	A	P
T	R	U	E	R		A	M	A
D	E	B	R	A		D	O	C
		C	O	N	T	A	C	T
S	I	R	I		E	R	O	S
T	R	A	C	I	N	G		
R	A	W		A	D	U	L	T
A	T	L		M	E	N	U	S
Y	E	S			R	S	V	P

page 6

A	N	T	S		U	P	S	A
L	I	A	R		R	O	O	M
E	L	B	O	W	B	U	M	P
C	E	L		H	A	N	E	S
		E	M	E	N	D		
A	S	T	A	R		S	I	M
S	P	A	C	E	T	I	M	E
T	I	L	E		E	G	O	S
I	N	K	S		A	N	K	H

page 7

H	A	L	L	S		S	A	P
E	A	S	E	L		I	C	E
R	A	D	I	O	E	D	I	T
			W	E	E	D	S	
		W	E	E	K	S		
O	P	E	R	A				
A	L	B	A	T	R	O	S	S
R	O	B		E	N	T	E	R
S	T	Y		R	A	C	E	S

page 8

D	R	A	T		J	E	W	S
R	A	J	A		H	A	R	E
I	C	A	N	T	E	V	E	N
P	E	R	T	I	N	E	N	T
			A	L	E			
S	M	E	L	L	A	R	A	T
P	A	R	I	S	I	A	N	S
A	Z	I	Z		K	I	N	K
R	E	N	E		O	D	E	S

page 9

D	E	B	T	■	S	E	T	S
I	M	A	M	■	P	L	O	T
C	I	C	I	E	R	E	G	A
E	L	K	■	L	E	A	S	T
■	■	T	I	M	E	R	■	■
O	H	A	R	E	■	N	U	N
B	O	X	E	R	C	I	S	E
O	W	E	N	■	U	N	D	O
E	L	S	E	■	E	G	A	N

page 10

A	C	A	■	K	I	N	D	A
L	A	D	■	I	M	E	A	N
A	R	M	■	W	O	O	D	Y
M	A	I	L	I	N	■	■	■
O	T	T	O	■	I	D	E	A
■	■	■	V	O	T	I	N	G
T	A	P	E	D	■	A	D	A
B	L	A	M	E	■	N	O	M
T	I	L	E	S	■	E	W	E

page 11

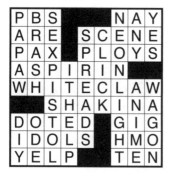

P	B	S	■	■	N	A	Y	■
A	R	E	■	S	C	E	N	E
P	A	X	■	P	L	O	Y	S
A	S	P	I	R	I	N	■	■
W	H	I	T	E	C	L	A	W
■	S	H	A	K	I	N	A	■
D	O	T	E	D	■	G	I	G
I	D	O	L	S	■	H	M	O
Y	E	L	P	■	T	E	N	■

page 12

M	A	G	■	■	L	I	P
E	N	Y	A	■	B	A	R	E
T	O	M	S	E	A	V	E	R
■	■	A	X	L	■	■
■	C	R	U	E	L	L	A
F	R	A	N	C	H	I	S	E
A	U	D	I	■	O	P	A	L
S	N	I	T	■	G	I	N	S
T	K	O	■	D	A	E

page 13

page 14

page 15

page 16

page 17

A	R	T				V	I	M
S	U	R	F		D	I	C	E
H	E	A	R		U	S	E	D
			O	R	B	I	T	
		G	H	O	S	T		
	S	L	A	N	T			
P	L	O	W		E	Y	E	S
B	A	R	K		P	A	L	E
S	P	Y				M	I	X

page 18

		G	E	E	S	E		
	B	A	L	L	E	R	S	
F	I	L	L	I	N	G	U	P
L	O	V	E	S	T	O	R	Y
A	B	A				N	E	T
U	R	N	S		G	O	S	H
N	E	I	N		I	M	H	O
T	A	Z	O		Z	I	O	N
S	K	E	W		A	C	T	S

page 19

C	A	L	M		N	C	A	A
A	L	O	E		O	H	M	S
M	A	S	A		B	E	E	S
	S	E	L	F	O	W	N	
		S	P	O	T	S		
C	E	L	L	P	H	O	N	E
F	L	E	A		E	V	A	N
O	M	E	N		R	E	A	D
S	O	P				R	N	S

page 20

C	B	S		A	M	I	S	H
L	A	W		C	E	L	I	A
O	B	I		A	T	L	A	S
V	E	G	G	I	E			
E	L	S	A		O	A	H	U
			B	U	R	G	E	R
V	A	U	L	T		L	A	B
A	T	S	E	A		E	V	A
L	E	A	S	H		T	E	N

page 21

S	W	A	B		G	A	L	S
K	I	L	O		O	N	I	T
E	L	L	A		O	K	R	A
W	E	I	R	D	F	L	E	X
		A	D	O	B	E		
B	I	N	G	E	A	B	L	E
O	R	C	A		L	O	U	D
D	E	E	M		L	O	N	G
E	S	S	E		S	T	A	Y

page 22

A	S	H				C	O	B
B	E	E		I	C	A	L	L
C	A	N	E	C	O	R	S	O
			P	E	G	L	E	G
	S	H	H		E	I	N	
S	H	A	R	O	N			
T	E	B	O	W	T	I	M	E
U	R	I	N	E		L	A	G
D	A	T				K	E	G

page 23

S	K	I	S		S	C	U	M
L	O	C	K		P	O	S	E
O	B	O	E		A	M	E	S
W	O	N	D	E	R	B	R	A
		A	V	E				
W	U	N	D	E	R	B	A	R
A	P	E	D		I	O	W	A
I	D	O	L		B	O	R	G
T	O	N	E		S	K	Y	E

page 24

S	P	R	I	G	S			
P	H	E	N	O	M	S		
R	A	T	T	L	E	R	S	
A	R	I		F	L	I	E	R
N	A	N	O		T	R	E	E
G	O	U	R	D		A	T	F
	H	E	A	D	A	C	H	E
		S	L	A	S	H	E	R
		B	Y	P	A	S	S	

page 25

A	S	P	S		A	H	E	M
T	H	A	T		T	O	D	O
M	O	N	O		E	G	G	O
S	W	I	N	G		H	E	R
		C	E	A	S	E		
F	U	R		S	T	A	T	E
I	H	O	P		O	V	A	L
D	O	O	R		R	E	P	S
O	H	M	Y		K	N	E	E

page 26

	K	G	B			W	C	S
S	N	E	E	R		I	R	K
W	I	N	T	H	E	D	A	Y
A	V	E		E	X	E	C	
M	E	A	D		T	A	K	E
	S	L	U	R		N	S	A
G	O	O	D	N	I	G	H	T
P	U	G		S	O	L	O	S
S	T	Y			N	E	T	

page 27

	M	A	I	D	S		
B	A	R	B	E	L	L	
F	L	A	M	E	O	U	T
F	I	B		P	E	C	O	S
		W	A	S	H	M	E
S	P	O	R	K		A	K	A
R	I	R	I		E	D	I	T
O	N	E	S		D	O	T	S
	T	O	T		O	R	E	

page 28

P	I	C	A	B	O		
O	U	R	L	O	R	D	
E	D	E	L	W	E	I	S	S
	P	A	L	O	O	K	A
A	L	E			R	I	P
P	O	P	D	I	V	A	
E	L	A	I	N	E	M	A	Y
	N	A	R	R	A	T	E
	L	E	A	S	E	S

page 29

T	U	B	A			S	T	O	W
I	D	O	L			A	R	I	A
M	O	N	E	Y	B	A	L	L	
E	N	D			E	R	N	S	T
		M	I	M	E	S			
S	H	O	V	E			L	A	O
K	E	V	I	N	C	A	S	H	
E	R	I	E			A	T	O	M
W	E	E	D			D	E	F	Y

page 30

H	A	R	S	H			M	E	D
A	L	P	H	A			A	P	R
L	E	G	A	L	I	Z	E	D	
				R	E	N	D	E	R
G	A	S	P			C	A	S	E
A	P	P	E	A	L				
M	A	R	I	J	U	A	N	A	
E	R	A			A	D	D	E	R
S	T	Y			R	E	S	E	T

page 31

B	B	C			P	R	A	Y	
O	O	O			R	E	E	S	E
S	H	A	K	E	R	A	T	O	
N	O	L	I	E			D	O	W
			I	X	N	A	Y		
P	O	T			A	I	M	E	D
S	T	I	R	C	R	A	Z	Y	
S	T	O	U	T			D	R	E
T	O	N	E				E	A	R

page 32

N	B	A				H	U	M
P	E	C	S			C	O	R	E
R	E	L	Y			O	U	I	S
		S	U	N	P	O	R	C	H
			O	A	K				
M	O	O	N	R	O	O	F		
E	N	V	Y			U	N	I	T
S	T	E	M			T	E	R	M
S	O	N				S	E	C

page 33

```
. . B U T T S .
S C O R I G A M I
P H O N E I T I N
L E G S . F I N D
A C E . . R U E
S K Y R . K I T E
H U M A N I Z E D
. P A R O L E S .
. . N E W T S .
```

page 34

```
V A T . A C U R A
E D U . C H A O S
R A P S H E E T S
S P A C E X . .
E T C H . M U C K
. . . U N I S O N
N E W M E X I C O
A R I E S . N O T
P A I R S . G A S
```

page 35

```
A B L E . A S H
H E I N Z . S P A
A D D T O . S A L
. . R O B E R T
F A C E M A S K S
L O R E A L . .
I R E . P L A Z A
E T A . P O L A R
S A M . T A P E
```

page 36

```
C O P . R O A M S
E V E . I N T R O
D U S T D E V I L
A L O N E . .
R E S T S E A S Y
. . H O W T O
S N O W A N G E L
P I X A R . E E K
A B O D E . E R S
```

page 37

page 38

page 39

page 40

page 41

```
    B A T
   N I C E R
  T A R T L E T
J U S T R E L A X
I N T H E P I N K
F A I R S H A K E
  S E A S O N S
    S T E N T
     E S E
```

page 42

```
L O T S     S A M
A B O U T   H I S
V E N M O   O M G
A Y E   O A R S
       T N T
S A W   A N G L E
A R I E L   A A A
M E T A L   M D S
E A S T     E Y E
```

page 43

```
    D D R
   B R I E R
  B E A C H E D
I R L M E E T U P
M I T E   A A V E
P O W D E R K E G
  N A I L S E T
   Y E M E N
    S O D
```

page 44

```
H O W L S   A S A
I D E A L   L A P
S E T S A D A T E
    H B O M A X
  N U B   J O Y
S O N A T A
M I C R O C H I P
O S U   S A U C E
G E T   S T E E P
```

page 45

D	R	A	T		S	E	N	T
O	U	C	H		A	L	O	E
F	L	E	A		U	S	E	D
F	E	S	T	I	V	A	L	
			S	C	I			
	O	F	L	I	G	H	T	S
S	I	R	I		N	E	I	L
O	L	A	F		O	R	E	O
B	Y	T	E		N	E	S	T

page 46

C	H	O	W		U	T	A	H
H	O	N	E		M	O	N	A
A	R	E	A		L	O	K	I
R	A	I	N	M	A	K	E	R
		S	A	U	L			
M	G	M		S	T	E	A	M
F	L	A	S	H	S	A	L	E
A	E	I	O	U		V	A	N
S	N	O	O	P		E	N	D

page 47

R	P	G		A	T	O	M	S
O	E	R		B	I	N	G	O
D	I	A	N	A	R	O	S	S
		N	O	S	E			
	T	H	E	D	U	K	E	
G	A	L	A		S	N	L	
I	R	A	N		W	H	O	M
L	E	N	D		P	E	W	S
D	A	D	S		M	R	S	

page 48

F	I	N			L	A	B	
A	C	E	S		C	A	M	E
N	E	W	T		O	B	O	E
		P	A	R	L	O	U	R
	P	A	R	K	O	U	R	
P	A	R	F	O	U	R		
O	L	E	O		R	I	B	S
G	E	N	X		S	N	A	P
O	S	T			G	A	Y	

page 49

O	D	D	■	■	■	H	A	M
T	O	E	S	■	T	U	N	A
I	R	S	A	G	E	N	T	S
S	K	I	L	O	D	G	E	S
■	■	■	A	W	L	■	■	■
U	S	E	R	N	A	M	E	S
M	A	X	I	■	S	A	V	E
P	L	E	A	■	S	I	A	M
S	E	C	T	■	O	M	N	I

page 50

I	T	E	M	■	■	A	V	A
S	I	R	E	E	■	L	A	B
M	E	R	R	Y	■	A	N	Y
■	■	■	L	E	A	R	N	S
C	H	R	I	S	T	M	A	S
P	I	A	N	O	S	■	■	■
L	S	D	■	R	I	N	G	S
U	S	O	■	E	G	Y	P	T
S	Y	N	■	■	N	E	A	L

page 51

O	K	S	■	■	■	E	R	A
M	A	T	H	■	I	V	E	R
G	R	O	U	P	G	I	F	T
■	T	A	B	O	U	L	I	■
■	■	C	P	A	■	■	■	■
■	F	L	A	U	N	T	S	■
W	R	A	P	P	A	R	T	Y
O	O	P	S	■	S	E	E	S
K	M	S	■	■	X	M	L	■

page 52

T	H	I	S	■	■	O	Y	L
O	M	N	I	■	■	F	O	O
W	O	N	D	E	R	F	U	L
■	■	■	S	E	L	■	■	■
■	H	O	L	L	I	S	■	■
L	I	A	R	■	A	M	O	K
A	S	S	T	■	X	I	A	N
S	A	T	■	■	T	K	O	■
T	W	O	■	■	S	S	W	■

page 53

```
D A N K   E N B Y
E L O I   N I L E
B U T D O C T O R
  M I D M O S T
      I A M
  T E E N P O P
P A G L I A C C I
G I G I   S H O P
A L O T   S O S A
```

page 54

```
F L O       B F F
U S S R   S E L A
S A L E S L E A D
S T O C K I N G
      R I M
  S T U F F E R S
S E M I F I N A L
P A N T   T V M A
A R T       Y I P
```

page 55

```
F A C E   B O O K
L I R A   I D L E
O D E S   K I D D
R E D E F I N E S
      S T N
M A G I C I A N S
A L A N   T R E K
A T I T   O L A Y
M O N O   P O L Y
```

page 56

```
S P A M   I P S O
P O L O   N O A H
A W L S   S L I M
R E B E L   A N Y
  R E S T A R T
A M T   R E B E L
T O T O   R E L O
O V E N   I A M B
Z E R O   E R O S
```

page 57

F	R	E	S	H		B	R	A
R	A	S	H	I		E	I	D
O	N	T	H	E	M	E	N	D
M	I	O			A	S	K	S
		N	A	M	E			
T	W	I	C	E		M	E	T
W	H	A	T	A	S	A	V	E
I	O	N		L	I	M	E	S
N	A	S		S	T	A	R	T

page 58

B	T	U		S	K	I	P	
R	O	N		L	A	N	E	S
E	R	E		I	R	E	N	E
E	N	T		G	L	E	N	N
Z	A	H	A	H	A	D	I	D
E	D	I	C	T		A	L	A
B	O	C	C	E		N	E	W
Y	E	A	R	S		A	S	A
	S	L	A	T		P	S	Y

page 59

L	O	O	P	Y		M	A	P
A	U	D	R	E		I	R	E
G	R	E	E	T	I	N	G	S
		W	I	G	O	U	T	
A	L	S	O		O	R	E	S
P	E	T	R	A	T			
T	W	E	N	T	Y	O	N	E
L	I	E		M	O	R	A	Y
Y	S	L		S	U	R	G	E

page 60

I		P	A	S	S		T	A	P
R	O	D	E	O		A	P	E
S	E	V	E	N		B	R	R
		I	G	L	O	O	S	
T	W	E	N	T	Y	O	N	E
T	R	A	G	I	C			
O	E	R		T	H	R	E	E
P	A	L		L	E	A	P	T
S	K	Y		E	E	N	I	E

page 61

```
. . S A I N T .
. I N B L O O M .
B L A C K S W A N
A L I . . . I R A
G O L D F I N C H .
. . . R I M . . .
G R E Y G O O S E
P A V E . F A U X
S E E R . F R E T
```

page 62

```
B U G S . . W O K
A T T I C . I K E
N A F T A . L A Y
S H O . L A D Y .
. . . M I C . .
A S H . I M A C .
C H A I N . R A D
D O I N G . D R Y
C E L S . . S E E
```

page 63

```
C A R . E X A M S
A L I . A R I E L
P O D . S A L L Y
R O O N E Y . . .
I F F Y . E D I T
. . J U D I T H
E L L E N . N A Y
G O T T I . E L M
G U E S T . D Y E
```

page 64

```
E R G O . Z I T .
D O O R D A S H .
U N D E R P L A Y
. . . U P E N D .
P O S T M A T E S
I D I O M . . .
P I M P E R N E L
. U B E R E A T S
. M A D . C H A D
```

page 65

```
S U M █ H O L D S
T S A █ U N I O N
E E N █ L E V E L
T U T T U T █ █ █
S P A S █ O A F S
█ █ H A N N A H █
C I V I C █ I R A
A D O R E █ S M H
D O N T S █ E S S
```

page 66

```
A D Z █ A P R I L
P R E █ L A P S E
H O L D T I G H T
I N D O O R █ █ █
D E A R █ O A F S
█ █ █ M U F F L E
B R E A K F R E E
I N A N E █ O C D
C A R T S █ S K Y
```

page 67

page 68

page 69

R	E	A	L	M		R	B	G
I	N	D	I	A		O	U	R
B	E	A	U	G	E	S	T	E
			I	L	E	N	E	
B	O	J	A	C	K	S	O	N
O	R	A	L	S				
B	O	W	L	E	G	G	E	D
U	N	E		T	O	R	T	A
P	O	D		S	T	R	A	Y

page 70

A	H	A		O	M	A	H	A
L	E	S		B	O	N	E	S
O	A	K	L	A	N	D	A	S
E	P	S	O	M		I	T	T
			T	A	P			
E	G	O		C	K	O	N	E
D	A	R	T	A	G	N	A	N
N	I	C	E	R		E	R	Y
A	T	A	L	E		A	C	A

page 71

			B	I	D			
		L	O	N	E	R		
	R	A	T	A	T	A	T	
L	A	S	T	M	O	V	E	S
O	N	E	L	I	N	E	R	S
A	D	R	E	N	A	L	I	N
	R	E	F	U	T	E	S	
		D	E	T	E	R		
			D	E	S			

page 72

		S	A	L	A	D		
	S	A	G	U	A	R	O	
R	E	P	E	C	H	A	G	E
Y	E	P			W	R	Y	
E	N	Y	A		K	N	E	E
		T	R	I				
W	E	B	I	N	A	R		
T	R	A	D	E	I	N		
F	A	Y		R	D	A		

page 73

```
    K A Z O O S
    A N I M A L
H U S B A N D R Y
A M O U R
T A L L C H I E F
    H A V R E
M I D W I F E R Y
A S S I S T
C H A N T S
```

page 74

```
S T A T   C U R B
A R C H   O R E O
M I N I B U S E S
  G E N E R A L S
    K A T
A I R F R Y E R
B R O A D A X E S
B I B S   R E N E
A S S T   D C O N
```

page 75

```
O H W O W   S E T
T I B I A   A M I
S C A N S   L I T
    K A M A L A
J O E   B I D E N
H A R R I S
E S A I   F A V A
R E S T   I P A D
I S E E   T E N D
```

page 76

```
D I P   R O C K
E G G   A U R A
F U R   I R A T E
Y E A R N   Z I N
  S T E   L I E D
  S I N G I N
I N N   O M E N S
L O G   J O S I E
K T S   I N S T A
```

page 77

page 78

page 79

page 80

page 81

E	T	C	H		S	T	A	R
D	O	R	A		A	C	T	I
G	R	O	U	N	D	H	O	G
Y	E	S	N	O		O	M	G
		S	T	R	A	T		
E	A	T		U	N	C	L	E
G	R	O	U	N	D	H	O	G
A	S	W	E		O	K	G	O
D	E	N	Y		R	E	S	T

page 82

D	O	U	G			P	A	T
A	R	S	E			E	L	O
M	E	E	T	S		A	L	P
			T	A	B	O	O	
S	U	P	E	R	B	O	W	L
A	P	O	L	A	R			
T	O	N	Y	D	U	N	G	Y
I	N	D			P	O	L	E
N	E	S			T	W	O	S

page 83

G	O	O	D	B	Y	E		
A	N	D	Y	O	U	A	R	E
S	T	E	E	L	G	R	A	Y
S	O	S		D	O	N	N	E
			S	M	S			
A	D	D	T	O		S	H	H
C	O	R	E	V	A	L	U	E
L	E	A	V	E	C	O	L	D
		B	E	S	T	B	U	Y

page 84

A	M	Y			S	E	W
W	O	O	D		F	A	T	E
L	A	K	E	H	O	U	S	E
	T	O	F	U	R	K	Y	
			E	N	D			
	P	O	N	C	H	O	S	
S	E	A	S	H	A	N	T	Y
P	O	K	E		M	E	A	D
A	N	Y			A	B	S	

page 85

E	L	L	A		H	E	L	L
N	O	O	N		O	B	O	E
D	O	G	G	I	E	B	A	G
S	P	O	R	T		S	N	O
		Y	A	O				
S	H	E		L	O	B	E	S
K	I	T	T	Y	H	A	W	K
I	R	O	N		E	B	A	Y
D	E	N	T		D	E	N	Y

page 86

Z	O	O	M		M	E	E	P
A	U	R	A		A	N	N	A
P	R	E	S	S	E	D	O	N
				E	V	O	K	E
J	O	H	N	L	E	W	I	S
O	P	I	U	M				
L	E	N	D	A	H	A	N	D
T	R	E	E		I	C	E	R
S	A	S	S		D	E	W	Y

page 87

W	I	I				P	A	Y
A	R	T	S		C	A	S	E
H	A	S	H	M	A	R	K	S
			A	I	D			
	S	U	N	B	E	L	T	
F	E	R	N		N	O	O	B
E	R	G	O		C	A	R	D
E	V	E	N		E	T	T	A
T	E	D				H	E	Y

page 88

L	E	D	I	N		R	S	S
E	V	E	R	Y		E	T	A
G	I	R	L	S		W	A	P
O	C	R		E	D	I	T	S
S	T	Y	E		A	L	E	
			M	A	I	D	S	
T	R	U	E	C	R	I	M	E
S	A	F	E	T	Y	N	E	T
K	N	O	T			G	N	C

page 89

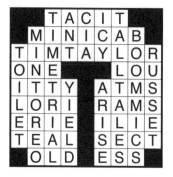

	T	A	C	I	T		
M	I	N	I	C	A	B	
T	I	M	T	A	Y	L	O	R
O	N	E			L	O	U
I	T	T	Y		A	T	M	S
L	O	R	I		R	A	M	S
E	R	I	E		I	L	I	E
T	E	A	L		S	E	C	T
	O	L	D		E	S	S	

page 90

R	A	M	I		D	E	C	K
A	L	O	T		E	L	L	A
H	A	N	S		E	B	A	Y
	S	A	M	S	P	A	D	E
		Y	E	S				
B	A	L	L	C	L	U	B	
E	L	O	I		E	P	I	C
A	S	O	F		E	T	C	H
R	O	M	E		P	O	S	E

page 91

X	I	N	G		A	P	E	X
T	H	E	A		F	I	L	M
R	O	X	Y		A	X	L	E
A	P	T	S		R	Y	A	N
			X					
T	R	A	M		Z	O	O	S
W	A	X	Y		E	X	I	T
I	C	O	N		R	E	L	Y
X	E	N	A		O	N	Y	X

page 92

P	B	S		S	A	N	D	M
O	A	K		C	R	I	E	S
P	H	I	F	E	D	A	W	G
		N	O	N	E			
		R	E	N	T	S		
G	U	R	U			I	P	A
A	T	O	M	I	C	D	O	G
G	A	S		S	H	A	R	E
S	H	E		M	E	L	T	S

page 93

```
S H E E S H ■ ■
F U S S P O T S ■
W H I T E H E A D
■ ■ ■ L O N G U
D I S C U S S E D
A L L A N ■ ■ ■
B L A C K F O O T
■ S T H E L E N A
■ ■ E R O D E D ■
```

page 94

```
A L B A ■ C O G S
D U L L ■ S O I L
O M I T ■ I F F Y
R E S A L E ■ ■ ■
E N T R Y F E E S
■ ■ B E F A L L
A L S O ■ E T T A
G E N Y ■ C M O N
E E L S ■ T E N T
```

page 95

```
A I D E ■ H U N G
C O O L ■ O H I O
T W O F O R O N E
S A M ■ U S H E R
■ ■ R T E ■ ■
S H R E D ■ E S P
T E A F O R T W O
U R G E ■ C O A L
D O U R ■ A N N E
```

page 96

```
■ C A P E R S ■
S H I R L E Y ■
T I M E S I N K S
O S E ■ E N D I T
P H D S ■ S I T A
S O F A R ■ C S T
■ L O S E F A C E
■ M R S M I T H ■
■ ■ Y O R E ■ ■
```

page 97

L	I	R	A			B	A	M
C	R	A	B		S	I	T	E
D	A	M	E	D	O	L	L	A
			E	F	L	A	T	
	V	I	P	P	A	S	S	
W	E	M	E	T				
K	N	I	G	H	T	L	E	Y
R	U	N	S		S	O	M	E
P	S	G			P	L	U	S

page 98

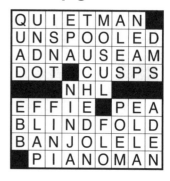

Q	U	I	E	T	M	A	N	
U	N	S	P	O	O	L	E	D
A	D	N	A	U	S	E	A	M
D	O	T		C	U	S	P	S
			N	H	L			
E	F	F	I	E		P	E	A
B	L	I	N	D	F	O	L	D
B	A	N	J	O	L	E	L	E
	P	I	A	N	O	M	A	N

page 99

S	O	F	T		A	C	H	E
I	G	O	R		B	R	A	Y
G	R	O	U	P	H	O	M	E
N	E	D		L	O	W	S	
		C	H	A	R	D		
	F	O	O	T		S	A	D
C	L	U	B	H	O	U	S	E
H	E	R	B		P	R	O	F
O	A	T	Y		I	F	F	Y

page 100

S	L	I	D		J	A	W	S
T	A	D	A		A	L	I	T
A	L	L	F	O	R	O	N	E
B	A	Y	O	U		E	S	P
			E	T	A			
H	I	M		D	A	N	C	E
O	N	E	F	O	R	A	L	L
U	R	G	E		O	P	A	L
R	E	A	D		N	A	Y	A

page 101

A	L	O	E			A	S	K
D	O	U	L	A		H	U	G
O	U	R	B	O	D	I	E	S
		S	O	L	E			
A	N	E	W		M	E	N	U
S	O	L		W	O	M	E	N
H	O	V	E	R		O	P	I
E	N	E	M	Y		T	A	T
N	E	S	T			E	L	E

page 102

L	A	C	E	S		S	T	Y
A	G	O	G	O		T	O	O
T	I	M	O	R		A	T	L
E	N	E		K	A	Y	A	K
	G	O	V	I	R	A	L	
		F	I	N	A	L		
A	M	F	M		B	E	E	F
F	O	I	E		I	R	M	A
T	O	T	O		A	T	O	M

page 103

O	F	F	R	E	D			
X	E	R	O	X	E	S		
C	R	E	E	P	I	E	R	
A	R	E		O	S	T	E	R
R	A	G	U		T	A	P	E
T	R	I	N	A		S	U	V
	O	F	F	W	H	I	T	E
		T	I	R	E	D	E	R
			T	Y	R	E	S	E

page 104

		F	L	A	P	S		
	P	R	O	P	E	L	S	
F	O	O	L	P	R	O	O	F
A	L	Y			M	S	U	
B	L	O	O	D	M	O	O	N
		H	O	E				
Z	O	O	M	G	L	O	O	M
I	O	W	A		T	U	N	A
T	H	E	N		S	T	E	P

page 105

E	C	O		C	H	E	E	R
B	A	R		H	I	N	D	U
B	R	E	V	I	T	Y	I	S
S	T	O	O	L		A	T	E
		W	I	T				
E	S	P		D	R	A	M	A
T	H	E	S	O	U	L	O	F
D	U	R	A	G		T	A	R
S	T	U	D	S		O	N	O

page 106

W	E	D		B	A	A		
A	G	O		I	F	I		
P	O	W	E	R	T	R	I	P
	N	E	D		S	T	L	
G	O	T	O	SEED		T	S	A
A	P	U			R	O	N	
P	E	R	M	A	N	E	N	T
	N	O	D	R	A	M	A	
	S	E	S	A	M	E	SEED	

page 107

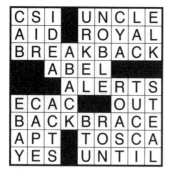

C	S	I		U	N	C	L	E
A	I	D		R	O	Y	A	L
B	R	E	A	K	B	A	C	K
		A	B	E	L			
		A	L	E	R	T	S	
E	C	A	C		O	U	T	
B	A	C	K	B	R	A	C	E
A	P	T		T	O	S	C	A
Y	E	S		U	N	T	I	L

page 108

A	H	E	M		A	B	C	S
C	O	M	A		R	O	L	L
D	R	I	P		E	B	O	Y
C	A	L	L	O	W	A	Y	
		E	W	E				
	D	A	L	L	O	W	A	Y
D	I	C	E		K	A	B	A
A	N	N	A		A	N	E	W
B	E	E	F		Y	E	L	L

page 109

I	L	S	A	■	M	C	A	T
B	E	A	T	■	E	R	I	E
M	A	L	T	■	T	O	M	S
■	H	E	A	D	R	U	S	H
■	■	S	C	O	O	P	■	■
W	A	L	K	T	A	I	L	■
I	D	E	A	■	R	E	P	S
R	E	A	D	■	E	R	G	O
E	N	D	S	■	A	S	A	P

page 110

B	B	C	■	S	E	C	T	S
O	E	R	■	A	L	O	H	A
B	L	A	C	K	F	L	A	G
A	L	F	A	■	■	O	T	S
■	Y	T	D	■	D	M	S	■
E	F	F	■	■	A	B	O	O
B	L	A	C	K	P	I	N	K
B	O	I	S	E	■	A	M	I
S	P	R	A	Y	■	N	E	E

page 111

F	M	L	■	■	■	C	O	O
L	A	Y	■	■	■	H	U	N
E	T	C	H	■	M	E	R	E
W	H	O	O	P	I	E	■	■
■	■	S	T	A	R	Z	■	■
■	■	B	R	A	W	L	■	■
I	N	T	O	■	C	H	I	P
R	U	B	Y	■	L	I	R	E
A	N	T	Z	■	E	Z	R	A

page 112

P	U	L	I	■	C	P	A	P
A	S	I	F	■	A	R	S	E
T	A	L	C	■	M	A	T	T
■	■	■	L	I	E	D	E	R
S	U	Z	A	N	L	O	R	I
E	N	O	U	G	H	■	■	■
R	I	O	S	■	U	T	A	H
I	T	M	E	■	M	I	S	O
F	E	S	S	■	P	E	K	E

page 113

T	R	Y		S	T	O	K	E
R	E	O		H	O	V	E	R
I	C	U		A	R	E	N	A
M	A	N	C	H	I	N		
S	P	A	R		E	M	M	A
	M	A	N	S	I	O	N	
S	U	E	D	E		T	U	G
E	F	I	L	E		T	R	E
T	O	T	E	D		S	N	L

page 114

B	O	D			A	L	T	
A	R	A	L		W	O	W	S
R	E	M	O		A	L	I	T
B	O	N	V	O	Y	A	G	E
			E	O	N			
S	E	A	S	H	E	L	L	S
P	A	R	E		S	O	O	T
A	S	I	A		S	A	G	A
	E	A	T			F	O	R

page 115

C	P	U		M	E	R	C	H
L	I	T		A	L	E	V	E
A	L	I		M	I	S	S	Y
S	O	L	O	A	C	T		
S	T	I	R		I	S	L	E
		T	A	G	T	E	A	M
P	R	I	C	E		A	R	I
Y	I	E	L	D		S	G	T
M	O	S	E	S		Y	E	S

page 116

O	P	T	S		S	H	O	T
L	O	O	N		N	O	D	S
D	O	D	O		O	H	O	K
S	L	O	W	Z	O	O	M	S
			B	O	P			
S	T	O	O	D	D	O	W	N
O	R	S	O		O	T	H	O
L	O	S	T		G	T	O	S
D	D	O	S		G	O	S	H

page 117

S	H	E			T	E	L
C	O	M	B		B	A	R	E
A	R	I	A		A	X	I	S
D	A	R	K	S	K	I	E	S
			L	E	A			
B	A	L	A	C	L	A	V	A
A	V	I	V		O	V	E	R
M	O	N	A		V	I	N	E
A	W	E			A	D	D	S

page 118

A	R	E	A		P	A	R
R	O	A	L	D		A	R	E
T	E	S	L	A		N	I	P
	Y	A	Y		D	E	E
N	I	G	H	T	F	A	L	L
A	G	O		R	I	B	
A	L	I		I	N	E	P	T
C	O	N		P	E	A	R	S
P	O	G		D	R	O	P

page 119

G	S	P	O	T		H	O	T
M	A	I	N	E		O	C	R
A	U	G	E	R		G	E	E
I	C	H		R	O	H	A	N
L	E	E		O	N	E	N	D
		A	O	R	T	A	
M	A	D	D		A	V	O	N
A	G	E	D		P	E	L	E
R	O	D	S		E	N	D	S

page 120

T	G	I	F		U	S	E	S
S	U	M	O		P	A	R	T
A	G	A	R		A	R	I	A
R	U	M	M	A	G	I	N	G
		Y	M	A			
T	W	O	S	P	I	R	I	T
H	O	P	I		N	A	D	A
E	V	E	N		S	T	E	P
M	E	N	S		T	E	A	S

page 121

O	K	S			L	O	G	A	N
O	N	E			O	H	A	R	A
F	O	R	T	W	O	R	T	H	
	W	I	I	G					
	N	F	C	E	A	S	T		
		R	A	I	N				
M	A	R	C	M	A	R	O	N	
A	L	O	H	A			E	T	A
T	I	E	I	N			D	E	B

page 122

S	K	I				O	C	H	O
E	O	N	S			I	R	A	N
T	I	G	E	R	L	I	L	Y	
		R	A	E		T	A	X	
	C	A	T	T	A	I	L		
A	H	I			I	B	C		
D	A	N	D	E	L	I	O	N	
A	R	E	A		E	S	P	Y	
B	O	D	Y			M	I	C	

page 123

I	C	Y				S	P	A
S	E	A			P	E	A	S
H	O	P	S	C	O	T	C	H
		K	A	L				
	F	A	I	L	L	E		
J	U	M	P	C	U	T		
I	M	E	D		T	H	I	S
V	E	N	A		E	A	S	E
E	D	D	Y		S	N	O	W

page 124

L	O	V	E	S	H	I	P	
P	O	I	N	T	E	D	A	T
S	H	O	R	E	W	A	R	D
		L	O	W		L	E	O
S	P	A	N		C	U	R	T
H	A	S		R	E	P		
A	N	O	M	A	L	I	E	S
D	E	L	A	R	E	N	T	A
	L	O	V	E	B	O	A	T

page 125

P	A	I	R			S/T	A	P
E	L	M	O		E	E	L	S
A	L	A	S		Y	A	M	S
S/T	A	M	E	N	E	S	S	
		H	O	G				
	S/T	W	I	R	L	I	N	G
Q	U	I	P		A	M	E	N
U	R	L	S		S	H	E	A
O	F	T			S	O	R	T

page 126

P	H	D			T	C	M	
T	U	R	F		A	R	Y	A
S	M	A	R	T	N	E	S	S
D	O	N	O	R		S	T	S
	R	O	M	A	N	C	E	
			V	E	E	R		
B	A	D	P	E	N	N	Y	
T	R	I	P	L	E	T		
W	E	R	E					

page 127

I	N	S	T	A		N	O	D
N	E	V	E	R		A	H	I
D	R	E	A	M		V	I	P
Y	O	N		Y	O	Y	O	
		B	R	B				
W	A	S		R	E	E	D	
E	X	T	R	A		A	R	T
P	L	A	I	T		N	O	R
T	E	R	M	S		S	P	Y

page 128

G	A	P	S		H	O	O	F
A	P	O	L	O	O	H	N	O
S	P	R	I	N	G	M	I	X
P	S	E	T	S		S	T	Y
			S	H	E			
A	M	A		O	G	A	W	A
W	I	N	T	R	Y	M	I	X
O	N	T	H	E	P	I	L	L
L	A	Z	Y		T	E	T	E

page 129

A	L	G	O	R	E		
S	E	A	R	A	C	E	
S	A	L	T	D	O	M	E
		H	A	L	I	T	E
A	L	G	O	R	I	T	H	M
N	E	A				T	O	O
G	E	S	T	U	R	E	S
E	C	S	E	G	A	R
R	H	Y	T	H	M

page 130

D	O	J		H	O	N	E	Y
I	P	A		O	L	I	V	E
D	U	C	K	T	A	L	E	S
	S	K	I	T		E	L	M
		P	O	T		
S	T	P		T	A	L	K
P	A	L	A	R	O	U	N	D
A	R	E	S	O		C	E	O
R	O	A	S	T		K	E	G

page 131

		B	E	A	R	H	U	G
I	L	L	M	A	N	A	G	E
S	E	A	C	H	A	N	G	E
H	I	D	E			
	S	E	E	S	T	A	R	S
		A	R	N	I	E
S	I	S	E	P	U	E	D	E
U	G	L	Y		S	T	E	M
B	A	R	E		T	A	R

page 132

M	E	L	A		M	E	L	B
O	V	E	R		A	R	I	A
P	I	N	T	G	L	A	S	S
S	E	A	C	O	A	S	T	S
			R	O	Y	
A	V	O	I	D	A	N	C	E
D	I	R	T	Y	L	O	O	K
A	C	A	I		A	M	I	E
M	E	L	C		M	E	L	D

page 133

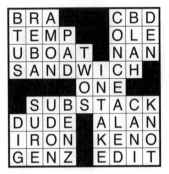

page 134

page 135

page 136

page 141

			I	T	A	S	C	A
	D	O	N	E	D	E	A	L
P	A	I	D	L	E	A	V	E
A	N	N	I	E				
P	O	K	E	M	O	N	G	O
				E	B	O	O	K
S	P	L	I	T	E	N	D	S
S	O	C	K	E	Y	E	S	
E	L	D	E	R	S			

page 142

	S	E	A	S	A	L	T	
B	U	N	G	A	L	O	W	S
E	N	E	R	G	E	T	I	C
A	B	M				U	T	O
R	A	Y				S	T	N
I	T	S				P	E	C
S	H	O	E	S	T	O	R	E
H	E	I	R	E	S	S	E	S
	S	L	A	C	K	E	D	

page 143

	R	E	D	L	I	G	H	T
A	I	R	C	A	N	A	D	A
S	P	R	A	Y	G	U	N	S
H	A	S				D	E	T
		M	C	L	Y	T	E	
A	S	C	A	L	E			
P	L	A	Y	A	G	A	M	E
R	E	M	B	R	A	N	D	T
	D	E	E	E	L	I	T	E

page 144

B	U	R	P		A	C	H	Y
O	T	O	H		P	R	A	Y
D	E	S	I		R	I	T	Z
	S	E	L	F	I	S	H	
	P	O	U	L	T			
S	H	E	L	L	F	I	S	H
A	U	T	O		O	A	H	U
F	L	A	G		O	N	I	T
E	L	L	Y		L	O	P	S

page 145

page 146

This grid indicates the letter S (which the grid resembles, and which starts every clue and appears in every answer, as noted by 11-Across.)

page 147

This grid indicates the letter E (which appears in every answer, and which the grid resembles).

page 148

This grid indicates the letter V (formed by a V-shape of V's in the grid, as shown above).

This grid indicates the letter E, the only vowel to appear in the grid.

This grid indicates the letter N (formed by an N-shape of N's in the grid, as suggested by 14-Down).

The grid indicates the letter D, per 15-Across.

The grid's theme entries both begin with OH, phonetically indicating the letter O.

page 153

V	E	T	S		E	D	N	A
O	R	E	O		L	E	A	N
W	I	L	D		W	E	S	T
S	E	E		P	A	P	A	S
		P	L	A	Y	S		
S	T	O	I	C		L	P	S
W	O	R	K		W	E	E	K
A	N	T	E		D	E	L	I
M	E	S	S		S	P	E	D

The pair of two-word phrases, in which each word starts with W, indicate the letter W.

page 154

BEE	C	H		B	U	S	Y	BEE
G	R	E		O	N	T	A	P
E	A	R		S	C	A	M	S
E	N	R	I	C	O			
S	E	E	N		L	A	F	F
			E	N	A	M	O	R
M	A	U	V	E		I	C	I
C	I	T	E	S		G	A	S
BEE	M	E	R	S		A	L	BEE

The starts of ENRICO and ENAMOR phonetically indicate the letter N. Together, the letters indicated by all nine puzzles spell SEVEN DOWN. Reading the initial letters of the clues for 7-Down in each puzzle reveals the phrase SPELLING B [bee].